COLD LIGHT

adapted by Alana Valentine
based on the novel
by Frank Moorhouse

CURRENCY PRESS
The performing arts publisher
www.currency.com.au

CURRENT THEATRE SERIES

First published in 2017
by Currency Press Pty Ltd,
PO Box 2287, Strawberry Hills, NSW, 2012, Australia
enquiries@currency.com.au
www.currency.com.au

in association with The Street Theatre, Canberra

Cataloguing-in-publication data for this title is available from the National
Library of Australia website: www.nla.gov.au

Typeset by Dean Nottle for Currency Press.
Cover design by Mike Jackson, DAMS design.
Cover illustration by Maria T Reginato.

Contents

Currency Press acknowledges the Traditional Owners of the Country on which we live and work. We pay our respects to all Aboriginal and Torres Strait Islander Elders, past and present.

Cold Light was first produced by The Street at The Street Theatre, Canberra, on 4 March 2017, with the following cast:

EDITH	Sonia Todd
MENZIES / SCRAPER / WHITLAM / WAITER / GEORGE / YIHZAR / PARTY GOER 2	Nick Byrne
AMBROSE / ASIO MAN / PARTY GOER 3	Tobias Cole
RICHARD / THOMAS / JOHN / VICTOR HALL / PARTY GOER 1	Gerard Carroll
GIBSON / FRED / TOCK / EISENHOWER	Craig Alexander
JANICE / AMELIA / WOMAN	Kiki Skountzos

Director, Caroline Stacey
Set Designer, Maria T Reginato
Costume Designer, Imogen Keen
Lighting Designer, Linda Buck
Sound Designer, Kimmo Vennonen
Movement Designer, Zsuzsi Soboslay
Voice Coach, Dianna Nixon

CHARACTERS

EDITH CAMPBELL BERRY

ROBERT MENZIES, Australian Liberal Prime Minister

AMBROSE WESTWOOD, Edith's husband and member of the British High Commission to Australia

RICHARD

TREVOR GIBSON, town planner

FREDERICK (FRED) BERRY, Edith's brother and Australian Communist Party (ACP) member

THOMAS, clerk in Gibson's office

SCRAPER, public servant

ASIO MAN, Australian secret security operative

JANICE LINNETT, ACP member

MR TOCK, member of the exclusive Melbourne Club

JOHN LATHAM, High Court judge

GEORGE T. MCDOWELL, mayor of Berry

AMELIA RICHTER, friend to Edith and Ambrose

GOUGH WHITLAM, Australian Labor Prime Minister

RICHARD VICTOR HALL, Labor Government Minister

YIZHAR, Israeli army colonel

EISENHOWER, US President

WOMAN, guest at Prime Minister's dinner

DELIVERY MEN

WAITER, The Melbourne Club

PARTY GOERS, ACP members

SPEAKERS, International Atomic Enery Agency (IAEA) Conference

CHAIRWOMAN, IAEA Conference

CAST

The cast compromises six actors (four male, two female) who double roles as follows:

EDITH

AMBROSE / ASIO MAN / PARTY GOER 3

GIBSON / FRED / TOCK

RICHARD / THOMAS / JOHN / VICTOR HALL / PARTY GOER 1

MENZIES / SCRAPER / WHITLAM / WAITER / GEORGE / YIZHAR / PARTY GOER 2

JANICE / WOMAN / AMELIA

SETTING

The action of the play takes place over twenty four years from 1950 to 1974 and traverses a series of locations including: The Lodge; a private suite at the Hotel Canberra; town planner Trevor Gibson's offices, Acton; a café in Manuka; the Melbourne Club; Berry Cemetery, NSW; Edith and Ambrose's home on Arthur Circle, Forrest; the Commonwealth Club; Edith's office, Acton; Hotel Canberra's Blue Room; Richard's home; University House, ANU; Parliament House lawns; Whitlam's office, Parliament House; Vienna, Austria; a hotel in Israel; Beirut, Lebanon.

This play went to press before the end of rehearsals and may differ from the play as performed.

ACT ONE

SCENE ONE: THIS LIFE-STREAM THIN

EDITH *stands alone on stage. She recites from the poem by Australian poet Adam Lindsay Gordon, 'The Rhyme of Joyous Garde':*

EDITH: Now I know full well that the fair spear shaft
        Shall never gladden my hand, nor the haft
          Of the good sword grow to my fingers;
        Now the maddest fray, the merriest din,
        Would fail to quicken this life-stream thin,
        Yet the sleepy poison of that sweet sin
          In the sluggish current still lingers.

> *Lights come up and the glamour, noise and vivacity of a cocktail party manifest around her.*
>
> *The Lodge, Canberra, 1950.*
>
> PRIME MINISTER MENZIES *goes over to* EDITH.

MENZIES: Adam Lindsay Gordon.

EDITH: That's right.

MENZIES: The only Australian poet in Poet's Corner, Westminster Abbey.

EDITH: In fact I know where Poet's Corner is, Prime Minister.

MENZIES: That's because you're clever, Edith. Clever enough to serve Australia at the League of Nations.

EDITH: To serve the world, sir.

MENZIES: Not clever enough to have prevented it from failing miserably, but then, we shouldn't associate you with its demise.

> AMBROSE *joins them.*

After all, you were clever enough to marry into the British High Commission.

AMBROSE: And now it is I who must correct you, sir, for it is she who condescended to marry me.

MENZIES: And if not for yourself, Major Westwood, then again I say, clever that in doing so she affirms that her security, her cultural existence and her love will always be with Britain, as will mine.

EDITH: Perhaps it is you who should have married him, Prime Minister.

MENZIES: If I had I would not allow him to force me to quote the mediocrity of Adam Lindsay Gordon.

> AMBROSE *snorts with laughter.*

Indeed I would not, sir.

AMBROSE: I am laughing, Your Excellency, at the preposterous notion of me being able to force Mrs Westwood into doing anything of which she herself is not the author.

MENZIES: How then do you explain her predilection for his verse?

EDITH: You're not an admirer?

MENZIES: The Archbishop of Canterbury thought I should be. When we met at a dinner very much like this one, at Neville Chamberlain's house. He told me that it was he who helped secure approval for the Poet's Corner bust and I told him that no good purpose was ever served by elevating the third-rate to the company of the great.

> *Beat.*

Will you take your seats?

> MENZIES *goes over to a table and sits down.* EDITH *keeps a smile fixed on her face as she speaks in a low voice to* AMBROSE.

EDITH: Well, what was all that about not blaming me for the demise of the League? Why would he say that?

AMBROSE: Perhaps you should take it at face value.

EDITH: Well, thank you for that nuanced reading of his political motives.

AMBROSE: He said three times how clever he knows you are.

EDITH: So why isn't he announcing my appointment to some government post in External Affairs?

AMBROSE: Perhaps he thinks you're enjoying just being home?

EDITH: Home is wherever he asks me to be this country's ambassador. He needs to make me Australia's first female diplomat.

AMBROSE: Well, he's not likely to if you keep trying to thrust me into his arms.

EDITH: He's reluctant now but wait till he sees you in heels.

AMBROSE: We should sit down.

EDITH: Who are you next to?

AMBROSE: Some sort of town planner. Apparently there's a new vision for Canberra. Which sounds absolutely terrifying. You?

EDITH: Someone called Richard. Seconded to a position on Menzies' new uranium committee.

AMBROSE: Stab him with the salad fork and then take *his* job.

EDITH: I may have to.

AMBROSE: When he asks you if you're missing the 'so-called' sophistication of Europe.

EDITH: And I tell him that in Canberra one can enjoy the privileges and discomfort of three modes of living in one place—the capital, the rural life and exile.

> AMBROSE *laughs. They both take their seats,* EDITH *facing out to the audience,* AMBROSE *behind the table, opposite* EDITH. *The* WOMAN *next to her smiles as she sits down.*

WOMAN: I love what you're wearing. It's Dior, isn't it?

EDITH: Thank you.

> *The* WOMAN *turns her chair 'in' to the table.* EDITH *turns to say hello to* RICHARD, *both with their chairs still facing the audience.*

RICHARD: She's right. It is a lovely suit.

EDITH: You have to look closely to see it's not a copy.

RICHARD: Well, copy or not, it fits you very well.

> EDITH *looks at him with interest.*

EDITH: Are you interested [*beat*] in fashion?

RICHARD: I especially like the idea of Parisian knickers.

EDITH: Do you mean Paris knickers?

RICHARD: Do I?

EDITH: I must say that it is quite indecent to be speaking to me about knickers when we haven't even been introduced, sir. I might wonder why you have the presumption to do so.

RICHARD: As I might wonder how you have the presumption to disagree with a newly elected Prime Minister to his face.

EDITH: 'Newly elected' being the operative words. I'd never try it when he'd been in office for some time.

> *They laugh.*

RICHARD: Still, it marks you out as a mutinous woman.

EDITH: Edith.

RICHARD: Richard.

EDITH: And what if I am a mutinous woman?

RICHARD: Then you know that in the case of Paris knickers, we are in fact talking about no knickers whatsoever.

EDITH: Yes, indeed.

RICHARD: So that when we turn to eat our lobster cocktail and our duck à l'orange, if I slipped my hand onto your leg and then moved it tentatively upward, pausing just a moment to thrill at the feel of the silk lining of your suit moving slightly against the silk of your stockings. If I did that would you edge your skirt up as far as you dared so that I could feel the smooth flesh of your leg between your stockings and your silk corselet. And would I, Edith, find that you are wearing the aforementioned Paris knickers which are in fact no knickers at all.

EDITH: You would.

RICHARD: Then perhaps we should turn and begin to enjoy our dinner.

EDITH: Alright.

> *But they do not turn.*

How did you know I wouldn't be scandalised by such a suggestion?

RICHARD: Are you?

EDITH: Absolutely.

RICHARD: Then why haven't you slapped me?

EDITH: I want to show you how much I know about uranium.

RICHARD: What do you know?

EDITH: I know that it has the symbol U and the atomic number 92.

RICHARD: Not enough to get a job, alas. You'd do better to talk to the town planner seated next to your husband.

EDITH: Do you think he'd like to hear my opinion on whether Canberra should have a lake?

RICHARD: While I'm only keen to splash my fingers around in any wetness I can find.

EDITH: Then by all means let's go paddling.

> *They turn, backs to the audience, to face the others.*

AMBROSE: Edith, I was telling Mr Gibson what a talent you have for plans and policies and plots.

GIBSON: Major Westwood seemed to think you might be able to help me with the diplomacy required in the designing of a new city.

EDITH: I am by background better suited to administration, Mr …?

GIBSON: Gibson. Would you like to help make the *caput mundi*?

At this point, RICHARD *finds her own* caput mundi. *She gasps.*

AMBROSE: He means the centre of things, Edith.

She looks at RICHARD *but he is absorbed in his dinner.*

EDITH: Then it is surely the *novum caput mundi*. The new centre of civilisation.

GIBSON: I accept the amendment.

EDITH: So you are planning the point around which all of Australia revolves?

GIBSON: I'm wanting to organise a congress. A regional and town planning institute conference.

EDITH: Canberra as the point from which Australia grows and flourishes, yes I see that.

GIBSON *takes out and hands her a card.*

GIBSON: I will give you my business card. Please telephone my secretary and arrange an appointment.

EDITH: I will.

AMBROSE: Shall we move to another position?

EDITH: Let's.

She looks at RICHARD *who stands.* EDITH *stands.* MENZIES, *the* WOMAN, AMBROSE *and* GIBSON *exit.*

RICHARD: I made you gasp.

EDITH: Mr Gibson made me gasp.

RICHARD: Oh?

EDITH: Offering to make me Mistress of the Capitolium.

RICHARD: I heard him say organise a conference.

EDITH: Then you were distracted.

RICHARD: And you weren't?

EDITH: Men think a sexual woman is not a serious woman when, in truth, the most focussed of us are frequently the most erotically fecund.

RICHARD *looks at her and exits.*

SCENE TWO: THE OUTERMOST BRINK

Hotel Canberra. The same evening.

EDITH *removes the coat of her suit and puts on a claret-coloured silk nightgown. She pours two glasses of port.*

AMBROSE *enters, wearing a matching negligée and nightgown.*

EDITH: A matching couple in claret silk.

AMBROSE: Where would a boy be without a silk negligée.

EDITH: It decidedly makes you unmanly, but I know you are thankful for that.

AMBROSE: That I am. Now what of this offer from the grand designer?

EDITH: The further we are from the party the less burnished the offer is looking.

AMBROSE: Any old position will keep your hands busy.

EDITH: I did not come back to Australia to organise a conference of town planning people who will talk about whether to put electric and telephonic lines above ground on poles or underground in concrete pipes. In Geneva we were disarming the world! We came this close to disarming it in '32. In Vienna I pulled displaced people from where they hid in sewers, shivering with fear. Organising a conference is not really my destiny.

AMBROSE: Then tell me again why we came to this place. I utterly do not know what we are doing here.

EDITH: Are you trying to provoke some degree of defensive patriotism in me? I can assure you my patriotism is very weak.

AMBROSE: Here we are in this diplomatically insignificant country, playing out petty imitations of distant places—the private schools are imitations, the parliament and courts are imitations. The whole place has insufficient identity or heritage or skills. You heard the PM say that the Communist Party is to be banned?

EDITH: We came here for me to be a diplomat and more. I seem to have misjudged how much I might be needed.

AMBROSE: And so we find ourselves in a rural outpost—on the border with the Gobi Desert. So let us despair. Let us despair awfully and enormously.

EDITH: We have never tried the life of the indolent rich.

AMBROSE: We could return to Geneva and I could work as a cigarette girl at the Molly Club. I wonder if Follett is still there pretending to be a dissolute old man while doing secret good works in expensive gowns and exquisite earrings. I envy his life. Must drop him a line.

EDITH: That too, my darling, we can find again. We can have that again if that is what you're missing.

AMBROSE: Oh, it's here, I suspect. In time it would show itself somehow, would wink at me some night, show its garter belt. Always does in whatever godforsaken country. Have not had a glimpse yet, truth be told.

> EDITH *goes to the butler's table and pours each of them another drink.*

EDITH: I have something risqué to tell—and for the telling we need a night potion.

AMBROSE: You do?

EDITH: A man at the PM's table put his hand upon my knee.

> *Pause.*

AMBROSE: And did he do it well?

EDITH: The climax of the gesture lacked what one might call a shapely conclusion.

AMBROSE: How so?

EDITH: After we rose from the table he made no further approach to me.

> AMBROSE *puts his hand under her dressing-gown.*

AMBROSE: But what did the hand do?

EDITH: It reached past the button of my suspenders to the flesh of my stocking top. And as you know there is then nothing between that and the corselet.

AMBROSE: I read that the corselet is on its way out. Sad. I feel sometimes that it braces me.

EDITH: I know precisely what you mean. A girl needs a little stiffening at times and you, I know, at times, my darling—need a little stiffening.

AMBROSE: Well, well. Well, well. A PM's dinner party—our first invitation to this Lodge, our most important social appearance in this capital—and you play hanky-panky under the table with a stranger.

EDITH: You are impressed?

AMBROSE: I am in thrall to you. You are naughty beyond all my highest expectations. I honour you. I worship at your feet.

> *He slides to the floor.*

EDITH: Then will you finish what the stranger's fingers began?

AMBROSE: My pleasure.

He parts her legs and buries his head between them.

EDITH: And when you are done I too shall steal my hand up your silken dress and introduce you to that ever stiffened implement we brought with us from Vienna. My pretty rubber penis for my darling nancy-man.

She gives herself vocally to the pleasure of his ministrations.

SCENE THREE: SOMETHING LIKE A WELSH MINER

EDITH *removes her dressing-gown and puts her suit coat back on. She straightens herself up when there is the sound of a buzzer.*

EDITH: I'm coming.

FRED *enters.*

Oh.

FRED: Good morning.

EDITH: Good morning.

FRED: Reception told me to come straight up.

EDITH: Yes.

FRED: You weren't expecting me.

EDITH: I was expecting room service but …

FRED: I'm your brother.

EDITH: Yes. I know who you are.

FRED: I thought … because I would have been …

EDITH: Seventeen.

FRED: [*simultaneously*] Seventeen when you last saw me.

EDITH: I know who you are. Come here.

They embrace. EDITH *is a little teary.*

Do you have a handkerchief?

FRED *pulls out a handkerchief.*

FRED: It's perfectly clean.

EDITH: Thanks for the assurance.

They laugh.

You disappeared from our lives. Tell me about you. How was your war?

FRED: I was overseas just after the war ended. Prague. I know about your position at the League of Nations.

EDITH: How did you end up in Prague?

FRED: The party sent me. A few of us went there for training. To see how a new communist state worked.

EDITH: And how did you find me?

FRED: I read about you in the paper.

EDITH: Oh, that newspaper article. I may have promoted myself up a level or two in the exuberance of the interview.

FRED: Yes, from my own research I'd say you definitely did.

Pause. EDITH *is a little thrown. He's been researching her. And he is letting the air out of her balloon.*

EDITH: But what are you doing in Canberra?

FRED: I'm in politics.

EDITH: How so?

FRED: I'm an organiser with the Communist Party.

EDITH: [*laughing nervously*] Rather an unpopular thing to be right now. I would keep it under my hat. Or cap in your case.

FRED: So … we're keeping it under your hat?

EDITH: In a manner of speaking.

FRED: Do you mean you will keep me a secret so that my beliefs don't blemish you?

EDITH: Well, I'm not sure if it's a secret job you're doing.

FRED: I judge the situation. Sometimes I am discreet, sometimes I am not, sometimes I am something else.

EDITH: He who fights for communism has, of all the virtues, only one— he fights for communism.

She laughs.

FRED: That amuses you?

She grabs his hand and squeezes it by way of apology.

EDITH: I'd like you to meet my husband, Ambrose. Are you married?

FRED: I have a friend. The Party's enough.

A silence.

EDITH: Well, a grand dinner next time. If a grand dinner can be found in this make-believe city.

He takes a piece of paper from his pocket and hands it to her.

FRED: You can leave a message for me on that number.

He exits. She looks at the paper.

SCENE FOUR: THE POWER OF ILL-DEFINITION

EDITH *recites from 'The Rhyme of Joyous Garde':*

EDITH: The deep dusk fires in those dreamy eyes,
    Like seas clear-coloured in summer skies,
        Were guiltless of future treason;
    And I stood watching her, still and mute,
    Yet the evil seed in my soul found root,
    And the sad plant throve, and the sinful fruit
        Grew ripe in the shameful season.

The Gibson offices in Acton. GIBSON *enters.*

GIBSON: You will not be a public servant. You'll be working in our offices at Interior.

EDITH: Mr Gibson, I've not yet accepted the position. What would I be doing?

GIBSON: Well, you'll basically take dictation. File documents, book rooms. Nothing grand. But you will liaise with the Secretary in Sydney and represent the department by delegation from me.

EDITH: That sounds more promising.

GIBSON: Oh?

EDITH: My boss in Geneva always told me that ill-defined positions carry a secret power. Those around such a person can never be sure where the person's authority ends.

GIBSON: I'd be happy for it to remain as elusively defined as you require.

EDITH walks around the room. She stops at the draughtsman's desk.

EDITH: What are these?

GIBSON: They are illustrations of Griffin's idea of Canberra—drawn by his wife we think. She was an architect too. I got them over from the Department of Works. They're a bit dusty. I wanted to have a quick look at them. I don't think they'll be much use.

EDITH: But these are magnificent.

GIBSON: I suppose they are good in a dreamy sort of way.

EDITH: I think it's more than that. They have a sort of geometric artistry.

GIBSON: Griffin would say a severe simplicity. He thought the city should look like a fine sculpture—pleasing when looked at from any angle. But these plans have been surpassed now. They were done before air travel, before everyone could own the motor car.

EDITH: I find myself frankly awed by them. Are you past that?

GIBSON: Well, I am left with the job of making the bloody things work.

EDITH: And then there's this lake.

GIBSON: The lake won't happen.

EDITH: Woodrow Wilson felt that a lake pacified the mind.

GIBSON: Not pacifying enough to stop the last war.

EDITH: I know something about the Garden City philosophy. I remember my father talking about those ideas.

GIBSON: An architect?

EDITH: A water specialist. He found water, he drilled bores. He was a maker of water tanks and dams, but he was also a thinker.

GIBSON: Well, don't get too attached to the lake.

EDITH: But why not? The idea of putting water into geometrical shapes. Perhaps it's art deco. But with room enough for fairies.

GIBSON: I beg your pardon?

EDITH: Lake fairies. Don't worry, I'm being playful. Lakes have fairies, I'm led to believe. Naiads.

GIBSON: What we need are more verticals, more variation of skyline, blocks of flats, spires.

EDITH: But the lake would bring fish and birds and nature right into the heart of our lives.

GIBSON: So is it our lives then?

Pause.

EDITH: A planner of the city deserves a special assistant.

GIBSON: Special assistant, is it?

EDITH: I accept the appointment and I would like to begin on my work today.

GIBSON: You'll need to meet my boss, McLaren.

EDITH: No, I don't think that's necessary.

GIBSON: He'll want to know that you *can* organise a conference.

EDITH: Let's just tell the Secretary of the Department of the Interior that I have hosted several picnics.

GIBSON: And let him think a picnic is a kind of European diplomatic event?

EDITH: In my hands it would be a diplomatic event.

GIBSON: You're not the least bit coy about your proficiencies.

EDITH: I pay you the courtesy of honesty, Mr Gibson. To Mr McLaren I would strategically conceal any ambition, initiative or even any semblance of an opinion.

GIBSON: You know him then?

EDITH: We were at university together. We met in the Science Society. He is quite the martinet.

GIBSON: And you will be Special Assistant going on Secretary of the Department?

EDITH: I suspect there are forms to be filled in before I can do that.

GIBSON: We'll find you a desk. You'll have to share.

EDITH: I work better in an office of my own. I'm a deep concentrator.

GIBSON: The position doesn't call for an office. Nor for a deep concentrator.

EDITH: I think it best for the appearances of the department and for the impression that you should make as Senior Planner of the city that I, as your special assistant, have a personal office.

> *He touches his hair.*

GIBSON: Well, we hadn't planned for anything more than a typist really.

EDITH: And yet here I am.

GIBSON: Yes.

EDITH: Ready to help formulate the ethos through structures and destine the nation.

> GIBSON *gives a small, uncertain nod.*

> *A clerk,* THOMAS, *walks past with a set of keys and a clipboard.*

THOMAS: [*to* GIBSON] Sign here.

GIBSON: I think Mrs Westwood will take responsibility for the key. Welcome aboard.

> GIBSON *exits.* EDITH *signs the clipboard for the clerk. He motions to leave.*

EDITH: Wait. I'll need a card. Edith Campbell Berry BSc Syd. Special Assistant to Mr Gibson.

THOMAS: I thought he said Mrs Westwood.

EDITH: Well, that is my married name. Campbell Berry is my professional name.

THOMAS: Okay. If you say so.

EDITH: And please add the office number and the telephone extension.

She shakes the keys.

THOMAS: I assume that will be a lady-sized card.

EDITH: No.

THOMAS: Then what?

EDITH: Make it the size men usually have their cards made.

THOMAS *looks her up and down and then exits.*

Around them other cast members move furniture into Edith's office. It need not all stay on stage, but she should be seen directing it into position. Finally one of the cast arrives with a cumquat tree. She gets them to put it in several different places before settling on a spot that is just right.

THOMAS *enters.*

THOMAS: Your cards.

EDITH: That was quick.

THOMAS: I told them that it was urgent and they should jump you up the queue.

EDITH: But the queue is one of the foundations of civilised behaviour, Mr …?

THOMAS: Thomas.

EDITH: We need to embody fairness and egalitarianism, Mr Thomas.

THOMAS: Not when you're a special assistant.

EDITH: Exactly so. For your reward, would you like a cumquat?

THOMAS: Can you eat them?

EDITH: Open up.

She motions to put the cumquat in his mouth. He pulls back.

You eat it whole, skin and all.

He takes the whole fruit into his mouth. Juice runs down the sides of his mouth.

You do not have to peel it. The sweetness is in the rind if it is a Meiwa cumquat, as this one is.

He smiles, chewing.

My mother's maiden name was Thomas.

He is still chewing.

We live our lives in our offices, Mr Thomas, and I intend to live in surroundings that please me. We all need *éclat* in our lives. Pizzazz. If I am to help design the ideal city, then that city begins [*with a gesture*] here in this room.

She looks down at her lovely wool carpet, as does THOMAS.

We need a place that greets people and shows them that Canberra people are different, or that those who live here will be changed, and that we are making something brand new here. We will be brand new people.

THOMAS *finally finishes the cumquat and swallows hard.*

A capitol is the memory of a nation. It is made up of records, photographs, books, paintings, films, relics, scientific specimens, its botany, its street names, its architecture. It's our desire to have our existence recorded and recognised by others. It is a way of eternal life, the only way, in my theological opinion. Not only soldiers but everyone. Everyone's name is here. Everyone's life experience will be here. Do you see?

THOMAS *nods at her, slightly dumbstruck.*

Now I really must get to work.

THOMAS: It's super, Campbell Berry.

EDITH: Oh, please. Call me Edith.

SCENE FIVE: THE COSTUMES MONEY WEARS

EDITH *works away on her desk as the lights change.*
She recites from 'The Rhyme of Joyous Garde':

EDITH: For the days recall what the nights efface,
           Scenes of glory and seasons of grace,
               For which there is no returning—

Else the days were even as the nights to me,
Now the axe is laid to the root of the tree,
And to-morrow the barren trunk may be
Cut down—cast forth for the burning.

SCRAPER *enters. He is crippled and walks with a pronounced limp.*

SCRAPER: Swank—*savoir-vivre.*

EDITH: Scraper. You're here.

He goes over to the Griffin plans.

SCRAPER: Planning Canberra, are we? A comedown from planning the world.

Pause.

EDITH: If you need financial assistance, I can help you a little.

SCRAPER: I do not need financial assistance, which, I take it, is what we'd call money. The acceptance of which would make me by definition a beggar.

EDITH: Money can wear a number of costumes. A loan, a gift, a guarantee.

SCRAPER: Buying someone off is another costume that money can buy. Blackmail too.

EDITH: What are you doing in Canberra?

SCRAPER: I am advising the War Memorial, insofar as they take advice. And meddling in affairs of state. The attractive thing about meddling, Edith, as you probably know, is that by definition you can do it uninvited.

EDITH: I have work to do, Scraper.

He stares at the plans and does not shift.

SCRAPER: Ha. Come over here. Look at this plan for the lake. It's there— the Eye of Providence.

EDITH *does not move.*

It's the same eye on the American one-dollar note. The all-seeing eye of God. But which god? This Griffin eye is surrounded by a small pyramid situated over a large pyramid. You've seen this mystical junk in these plans?

EDITH: What mystical junk?

SCRAPER *explodes with fury.*

SCRAPER: Geomancy.

EDITH: In Griffin's plans?

SCRAPER: Numbers and ratios and progressions of triangles ever larger. Magical sequences. And by manipulating the structures they can manipulate us. With the occult. Come and look.

EDITH: I'm hardly going to give you that satisfaction.

SCRAPER: He's playing with earth, water and air. But where is fire? Unless. Of course, the trees. He's deliberately exposing the city to fire by planting a bushfire within it. Trees are really torches of the gods. Tell me if they were theosophists.

EDITH: I have no idea.

He moves closer to her.

SCRAPER: Then find out and we'll have a drink. Or you can come to my room at the Kurrajong.

EDITH: Do you think you can use your war injuries to try and bully me, Scraper? I'm sad for you, but I am not going to be bullied by you.

SCRAPER: Oh, but I think you will.

He moves across and tries to kiss her. She pushes him off and he doesn't resist her rejection. But it is an uncomfortable moment. He moves to the cumquat tree, takes a handful of soil, throws it into the air and watches it fall to the floor.

Study the fall of the soil, E. Read the geomancers. Know who they are.

But now EDITH *loses her temper.*

EDITH: Even if there is a sort of symbolism in the planning, how would it ever affect those who live here?

SCRAPER: Beware of anything that has a cross at its heart. And this city has a cross at its heart. The cross is one of the most ancient symbols, probably the first symbol. Probably the first human construction.

He breaks two twigs off the cumquat.

We tied two sticks together, and hey presto—magic. Thus the division of the world into four elements and four cardinal points. And some still hold to the primitive power of what the first humans felt.

Pause.

The Red Cross had better change its name or Menzies will ban it.

She smiles.

Ah yes, the brother. Of course.

He grabs the maps and carries them over to a chair, spreading them over himself like a sheet.

They have made Capitol Hill the phallus of the Australian universe. The religious churches are pushed out of the sanctified triangle and will be replaced by secular temples. The Temple of Knowledge, The Temple of Justice, The Temple of Art. They think that their plan contains within it a higher stage of human spiritual development, which will suppress the maladies of modern civilisation.

He is masturbating under the plans, using them to relieve himself.

EDITH: What are you doing?

SCRAPER: Even the streetwalkers will not take me. I frighten them.

EDITH: Someone could come in.

SCRAPER: While you're allowing it.

EDITH: I'm not.

SCRAPER: You're allowing me to imagine you, exposed in your lingerie.

He stands up and, still holding the plans between them, rubs himself on EDITH, *in an act of vigorous frottage.*

EDITH: Don't do this.

SCRAPER: Don't do this again.

EDITH: Scraper, please.

SCRAPER: 'Please don't reveal my enfeebled will, please don't show me my own salacious compliance.'

EDITH: Stop it.

SCRAPER: You stop it.

EDITH: I can't.

SCRAPER: Why?

EDITH: I don't know.

SCRAPER: You still don't know. You still don't know why it happened all those years back.

EDITH: I still don't know.

SCRAPER: You still don't know why you're now wet, and you still don't know why your body is behaving in what you think is a lewd way.

EDITH: Stop it.

SCRAPER: When I leave, you'll be in a silent rage that you let it all happen again. As you are now in a cold horror that you want to participate. Vulva. Phallus.

EDITH: No-one has this over me. No-one controls me now, Scraper. No-one.

SCRAPER: Someone.

EDITH: No-one.

SCRAPER: Yes.

EDITH: No.

SCRAPER: Yes.

EDITH: No.

SCRAPER: Yes. Yes. Yes.

He climaxes, grunting, with eyes closed.

Thank you.

EDITH: Get out.

He does up his flies.

SCRAPER: You might ponder the power of physical ugliness. Of ugliness in general.

EDITH: I won't.

SCRAPER: No?

EDITH: No. Because the sexual does not matter. It does not matter a damn.

SCRAPER: The attitude of a whore.

EDITH: So be it.

SCRAPER: No-one need ever know.

EDITH: No-one will ever know.

SCRAPER: Not even dear Ambrose.

SCRAPER exits.

SCENE SIX: MISTER SPOTLESS

The ensemble sings the last verse and chorus (or more as required) of the Stephen Foster song 'Hard Times Come Again No More'.

The cumquat tree is broken, the fruit has been stripped from it and stamped into the rug. 'RAT' is written in red all over the wall behind EDITH. *She sets right the cumquat trunk and, in silence, crying, binds it with her handkerchief.*

THOMAS *enters. He is distressed by the damage to the tree. He looks at the wall.*

THOMAS: Oh no, not our lovely beauty.

EDITH: Who would have done this?

THOMAS: Well, the word 'rat' has at least three meanings I can think of. To be a betrayer, to be a cad and to be a communist.

EDITH: There's one you've left out.

THOMAS: Oh?

EDITH: To be a hairy rodent.

THOMAS: No, I'd say someone thinks you're a communist.

EDITH: What makes you say that?

THOMAS: Some people think the League was a communist plot. You have more books in your office than most and you're an atheist.

EDITH: Am I?

THOMAS: Never seen at church. And again I say, too many books.

> *He exits.* EDITH *picks the cumquats up and puts them in an envelope.* THOMAS *re-enters with a bucket of hot water and a brush.*

Here, splash that on the stain.

EDITH: You're a marvel.

THOMAS: I'm something of a Mr Spotless.

EDITH: Thank you.

> *Pause.*

Do you think my bandage will work?

> THOMAS *pulls tape from his pocket.*

THOMAS: I've got some Scotch tape from the head clerk's secretary. I don't think you're entitled to it.

> *He ministers to the tree.*

There is of course another possibility.

EDITH: No, I'd say communist is the most likely explanation.

THOMAS: Well, I hear you have a house.

EDITH: Does everyone in the world know I've been allocated a house?

THOMAS: In the world of Canberra, it's an event for someone to get a house.

> *Pause.*

EDITH: As it happens, I do have a communist brother.

THOMAS: Yes, I know. I've spoken to him.

EDITH: When?

THOMAS: There are communist members in this department.

EDITH: There are?

THOMAS: Yes.

EDITH: But not you?

THOMAS: No.

> *Two* DELIVERY MEN *enter, both carrying cumquat trees.*

EDITH: What's this?

DELIVERY 1: We're from the nursery. Where do you want them?

THOMAS: This is ridiculously fast, boys, better not keep this up or someone will think we're in private enterprise.

> EDITH *signs a clipboard and points to the other tree.*

I ordered one as a companion for the sick tree.

DELIVERY 2: This one's been in the wars.

> *He pushes his finger in the soil, picks a leaf, breaks it and smells it.*

It'll live.

EDITH: Who can the second tree be from?

DELIVERY 1: Ah, the second order is from a Mr Gibson.

DELIVERY 2: Yeah, I heard the villain is a nutty clerk in motor vehicle licencing. So if I've heard, Gibson's heard.

THOMAS: If Gibson's heard the story, it's all over the Acton Peninsula.

> *The* DELIVERY MEN *exit.*

EDITH: Quite the notorious woman. No matter. I shall embrace it with enthusiasm.

THOMAS: You'll be a protected person. Once Mr Motor Licence Man hears he won't touch your trees again, and he won't be getting a promotion.

EDITH: I have no idea Gibson had so much power.

THOMAS: You know that the department is pretty much split on the bill to ban the communists.

EDITH: I'm for the Declaration of Human Rights. The bill infringes it. I am not pro-communist.

THOMAS: Says the notorious woman with her trees full of ripe red fruit.

They laugh.

A MAN *appears.*

ASIO MAN: Excuse me?

EDITH: Yes?

ASIO MAN: Are you Mrs Edith Westwood, also known as Campbell Berry?

EDITH: Yes.

ASIO MAN: May I have a word with you?

EDITH: Yes.

ASIO MAN: Privately. It's a matter of national importance.

EDITH: I'm told it will live.

ASIO MAN: Sorry?

EDITH: You're not here about my cumquat?

ASIO MAN: No.

THOMAS: [*waving the tape*] If you need to bind anything else with Scotch tape, let me know.

EDITH: Thanks.

THOMAS *exits.*

ASIO MAN: As the wife of a diplomat you are covered by immunity, although if something serious were alleged you and your husband could be asked to leave the country.

EDITH: Excuse me, but who are you?

ASIO MAN: I'm from the new security services.

EDITH: The ASIO?

ASIO MAN: Yes.

Pause.

EDITH: I come back to Australia to offer my services, and now that I am offering them, in this albeit very humble way, you treat me as a traitor?

ASIO MAN: What makes you think we see you as a traitor? We may want to enlist your help.

EDITH: With what?

ASIO MAN: Your brother is a paid organiser of the Communist Party of Australia?

EDITH: You do know that Australia is a signatory to the UN Charter on Human Rights.

ASIO MAN: We are signatories but it is not law, in Australia. May I ask if you see your brother often?

EDITH: You may not.

ASIO MAN: Are you also a member of the Communist Party?

EDITH: No.

ASIO MAN: Are you a member of the secret branch of the Communist Party?

EDITH: If I were, would I have said yes?

ASIO MAN: It doesn't perturb you? As the wife of a British diplomat? Mixing with that type of person?

EDITH: I don't have any secrets to pass on.

ASIO MAN: You may not know you are passing on secrets.

EDITH: What I know or don't know about people is not your business, unless they are breaking the law.

ASIO MAN: You are opposed to religion.

EDITH: I fail to see the relevance.

ASIO MAN: It appears that your father had a non-religious funeral.

EDITH: He had a rationalist funeral. I wasn't there.

ASIO MAN: Rationalist, anti-religion is the same thing.

EDITH: I thought that since the French Revolution we are not held responsible for the crimes of our relatives. If being a rationalist and anti-religion can now be construed as a crime.

ASIO MAN: I find it curious that you did not attend either your mother or your father's funeral.

EDITH: My mother wished me to stay at my post with the League of Nations rather than make the trip home. My father died during the war and I couldn't find transport to Australia. And seeing that you are so keen about the matter of death, rationalists do not place the same emphasis on it as, say, religious people do.

He is writing in his notebook.

ASIO MAN: I shall put that in my report.

EDITH: Who sees your report?

ASIO MAN: Those authorised to see it.

EDITH: The PM?

ASIO MAN: If he wishes to.

EDITH: I am far from happy about this.

ASIO MAN: Then I advise you to avoid contact with your brother and any of his friends. One is not required to keep company with those who pose a risk.

EDITH: And I advise you to stay away from me until you have evidence that I am engaged in activities that threaten the security of the nation, and until you have evidence that myself or my family have taken actions that constitute a crime.

ASIO MAN: This is not an argument over politics. This is a polite interview to alert you to risk. And to see if you would be prepared to tell us anything you find out that could be of interest.

Pause.

EDITH: You want me to pass on information.

ASIO MAN: If it is useful.

EDITH: About my brother's … activities.

ASIO MAN: That's right.

Pause.

EDITH: I will take it under consideration.

ASIO MAN: You will?

He looks at her. She turns from his gaze, guiltily.

He exits. Behind EDITH *the ensemble play a kind of hide and seek game. One following another and hiding and then revealing. A sense of people being watched and watching. Finally one of them surreptitiously makes her way over to* EDITH.

SCENE SEVEN: SOME SUGGESTION OF PASSION

A café in Manuka.

JANICE: Do you mind if I join you?

EDITH: I'm waiting for someone.

JANICE: You're waiting for Fred, your brother. I'm Janice.

EDITH: His friend.

JANICE: That's right.

EDITH: Is Frederick still coming?

JANICE: He'll arrive after me to check that we're not being followed.

EDITH: Is that really necessary?

JANICE *checks over her shoulder, left, then right, then looks at* EDITH.

JANICE: Are you intending to join our protest outside Parliament House?

EDITH: You're talking about the Prime Minister's bill?

JANICE: To ban the Party. Of course I am. You knew that. Can't you give a straight answer?

EDITH: No.

JANICE: No, you're not joining us. Have you been given reserved seating passes for the diplomatic gallery, then?

EDITH: Yes. How could you know that?

JANICE: You're a diplomat's wife.

EDITH: I have an independent opinion.

JANICE: Really? Would you let me borrow your pass, then?

EDITH: To do what?

JANICE: To print up a few hundred and infiltrate.

EDITH: And what about when it is traced back to me and I go to gaol for it?

JANICE: All police leave in New South Wales has been cancelled. Sydney police are being driven here in government buses. We'll all be going to gaol is this bill goes through.

    Pause.

EDITH: The passes are under lock and key at the High Commission. It's an unfair ask.

JANICE: Is it? On the night of the bill you will be hobnobbing with people who want to put your brother and me in gaol.

EDITH: It is the nature of civility that we learn to mix in an easy way with those with whom we do not agree.

JANICE: You know you'll have to cross the picket line. In your furs and pearls. I'll be watching for you. And so will Fred.

EDITH: Where is Fred?

JANICE: Not coming. Something more urgent to do, I expect.

EDITH: Did he send you to try and persuade me?

    JANICE *reaches across the table and holds her hand.*

JANICE: Are you likely to be more open to my persuasion than his?

EDITH: Did he say that?

JANICE: Let's stop talking about him.

EDITH: Janice.

> JANICE *reaches up and touches* EDITH *'s face.*

JANICE: Perhaps you want to look at what is on the other side of the barricade?

EDITH: I don't know what you mean.

JANICE: Yes, you do.

EDITH: Yes, I do.

JANICE: I think you've been this close before. Am I right?

> *Pause.*

EDITH: I think you're presuming a lot.

JANICE: It's astonishing how quickly you can pick up on the signals of others, if you're open to them.

EDITH: I didn't give you any signals.

JANICE: Who?

EDITH: Me.

JANICE: You mean Edith. Well then, let me make it easier for this part of you that is … interested. I can call you something else. Like Eddie.

EDITH: What?

JANICE: You've never had the courage to be open to … what you know you want. But courage can be in a name. If it's not Edith then it can be Eddie or Edward. Ted or Teddie.

EDITH: I'm very flattered, of course.

JANICE: Or maybe you'd like me to call you Fred, or Freddie. To give it a nice little incestuous edge.

> EDITH *looks at her.*

Go there. You'll be glad.

EDITH: [*emphatically*] No.

JANICE: Then stop pretending it's a possibility and you're not just a conservative little diplomat's wife, after all.

> JANICE *stands. She is joined by the other ensemble members who perform a kind of Soviet dance routine as she sings 'Which side are you on?', a Depression-era workers' song later made famous by Pete Seeger:*

[*Singing*] Come all you good workers
  Good news to you I'll tell

Of how the good old union
Has come in here to dwell

Which side are you on?
Which side are you on?
Which side are you on?
Which side are you on?

Don't scab for the bosses
Don't listen to their lies
Us poor folks haven't got a chance
Unless we organise.

SCENE EIGHT: WHAT FRESH HELL

The voice of MENZIES *as* EDITH *and* AMBROSE *dress for Parliament at their Forrest residence.*

MENZIES: This is a bill to outlaw and dissolve the Australian Communist Party, to pursue it into any new or associate forms, and to deal with the employment of communists in certain offices. The bill is admittedly novel and it is far-reaching.

AMBROSE *hands her the pearls.*

EDITH: I'd rather not.

AMBROSE: We must not displease the Crown.

MENZIES: It is designed to give the government power to deal with the King's enemies in this country.

EDITH: It's not an opera.

AMBROSE: Oh, yes it is.

EDITH: You always want me to dress how you would dress.

AMBROSE: Precisely.

MENZIES: For some years, I and other persons resisted the idea of a communist ban on the grounds that, in a time of peace, doubts ought to be resolved in favour of free speech.

EDITH: My brother is going to be out there with the masses.

AMBROSE: How many does it take to form a mass?

EDITH: I don't agree with this bill.

AMBROSE: And nor do I. I'm calling it the banishings and huntings bill. If there's another war, banishing the communists here is not going to stop it.

EDITH: Then we should be out there.

AMBROSE: Really? I don't think so, Edith. You belong *in* the conversation.

EDITH: I know, but I can't *get* into the conversation.

AMBROSE: But you will.

EDITH: How? I thought the Public Service marriage ban, forcing women who get married to resign, I thought that was something they wheeled out to justify getting rid of women they didn't want. I thought the obstacles would be overlooked or waived away for the really deserving. You don't fill the gaps in Australia's skills by pointing to the gap between a woman's legs.

AMBROSE *laughs.*

What?

AMBROSE: We can leave.

EDITH: Do you know what it's like to know what you're capable of but never find a way to offer it? This is not about my personal ambition, my personal significance. This is about knowing that I was born to help Australia lead the world to peace. Evatt knows it about himself. People know it about themselves. I know it about myself. International peace seems impossible. Nuclear weapons are making the future seem impossible. But if I was asked, I could make a difference, I could. I have the vision.

AMBROSE: There's no-one who believes it more than me.

EDITH: You indulge me.

AMBROSE: Not at all. I love you and I respect you. But more than that, I see you.

EDITH: So why can't they?

AMBROSE: Too busy looking under the bed for reds.

MENZIES: We are not at peace today, except in a technical sense. The Soviet Union has made perfect the technique of the Cold War. The real and active communists in Australia present us with our immediate problem. Not the woolly-headed dupes, not the people who are pushed to the front in order to present a respectable appearance. Can we recognise and deal with the enemies of liberty only when they actually take up arms? What liberty should there be for the enemies of liberty? I am now going to read the names of fifty communists and their elected positions in the unions.

AMBROSE *and* MENZIES *exit.*

FRED *and* JANICE *enter.*

FRED: It's law.

JANICE: We are officially members of an unlawful association. Our property forfeited without compensation. Trade unions declared as communist affiliates, prejudicial to Australia's security and defence.

EDITH: There will be a High Court challenge.

JANICE: Latham will give them what they want.

EDITH: No. You're wrong. Justice Latham was a mentor. He may hate you, but he knows the Constitution. Parliament can only proscribe organisations when we are in a state of war.

JANICE: Menzies says that he'll put it to a referendum.

EDITH: Which will never succeed.

FRED: We are talking about Queenslanders. And Western Australians and Tasmanians.

EDITH: You're paranoid.

FRED: I say again, it's law.

JANICE: And they'll crack down immediately.

FRED: Listen. We have a plan that involves you.

EDITH *paces. Then nods.*

We need to store our records and files somewhere, until the matter is resolved one way or another.

JANICE: You're above suspicion and Ambrose gives you diplomatic immunity. They can hardly raid the house of an English diplomat, so no-one is really at risk.

EDITH: And if they did raid us?

JANICE: Menzies licks the boots of England—wouldn't do it.

EDITH: But if it did happen I would be arrested and Ambrose would be sent back to England.

JANICE: His diplomatic status would extend to you. They couldn't arrest anyone.

EDITH: You must accept that by now the Security Intelligence Organisation knows about our connection?

FRED: They know but they cannot act.

EDITH: And what happens when the Party is banned and you two have to flee to Russia? What happens to the records then?

FRED: Our flat has been compromised, Edith. We can go underground and operate clandestinely, but not yet. It will be in place in a week or so and then we can retrieve the boxes.

EDITH *paces.*

EDITH: I will not do it for the Communist Party. I will do it because I think you are both decent. And I do not want either of you to go to gaol. I will do it because I oppose this legislation and the thinking behind it.

FRED *and* JANICE *nod and exit. They carry boxes onto the stage and pile them up. They continue doing so during the following scene, building and shaping them into a city skyline in silhouette.*

The ensemble performs the song 'Sweet Violets', a big hit for Dinah Shore in 1951 (which is when the following scene is set).

SCENE NINE: PROTÉGÉE NO LONGER

The Melbourne Club, 1951.

JOHN LATHAM *and* EDITH *stand, having sherry, when a man,* MR TOCK, *comes over to them.*

TOCK: Hello, John.

JOHN: How are you, Tock?

TOCK: Won't you introduce me to this lovely young lady?

JOHN: I will introduce you, but I should warn you that we have some private matters to discuss.

TOCK: Something to do with your having 'deferred to the Parliament' on the communist ban, I hope.

JOHN: The defence powers clauses of the Constitution justify my decision to uphold the legislation.

TOCK: Not what your fellow High Court judges thought.

EDITH: Hello, I'm Edith Campbell Berry. Justice Latham was my mentor.

JOHN: Wife of Major Westwood from the British High Commission.

TOCK: I see. Then I suppose you agree with him that they should have banned the communists. Well, I for one am glad they didn't.

JOHN: Nice to see you, Tock.

TOCK: A pleasure to meet you, Mrs Westwood. Don't take any notice of me. My family were only one of the founding members of this club.

We donated the clock in the entrance hall sometime in the last century. Not that anyone remembers you for having given a clock.

TOCK *exits.*

JOHN: You must be very cross.

EDITH: Must I?

JOHN: Justice Latham was my mentor. Past tense.

EDITH: I am more disappointed than cross. I assured someone that you would never vote in favour of the ban. And then you did.

JOHN: You're going to tell me why that was wrong.

EDITH: I thought you could have leaned toward the Universal Declaration of Human Rights. That we should now lean that way whenever the situation allows it. I see it as a higher constitution.

JOHN: The case was about the power of the parliament. It wasn't about the Universal Declaration.

EDITH: But surely it was underlying everything that was argued in the case. The Declaration must have been in your mind and in the minds of the other judges. Freedom of expression, free association, peaceful assembly, freedom from want and fear.

JOHN: The Declaration has not been signed into our law. Cabinet simply ratified it. You should understand that.

EDITH: Even the War Memorial's new main sculpture will symbolise the four freedoms.

JOHN: I believe Menzies is right when he says that within forty-eight hours of the Third World War breaking out we would have communist militias in this country.

EDITH: It's only when war breaks out and they take up arms that we should be putting them in gaol.

JOHN: After war breaks out it might be too late to gaol them.

EDITH: But you're ignoring that we live under two constitutions now. The National Constitution of Australia and the Universal Declaration of Human Rights.

JOHN: A ratified agreement is a non-binding instrument. It is still not law.

EDITH: John—I spent twenty years of my life with the League. I know about treaties and non-binding instruments. But the Declaration at least represents a universal *vœu*, a wish. It is intrinsic to the human condition. An accepted standard of world behaviour.

JOHN: Somewhere between a hope and a dream.

> *Pause.*

Shall we to table?

> *A* WAITER *pulls out their chairs and they sit down.*

EDITH: We do not know when a desire, a dream, a *vœu*, can spring to maturity and become a commanding political reality.

JOHN: It is the timescale that matters. Will it be reality next month or next century?

> *The* WAITER *drapes napkins over their laps. With* EDITH*'s he seems to linger, drawing the napkin across her lap first and then placing it in place.*

EDITH: To know if something is before its time it has to be tested and re-tested.

JOHN: We'll have the Nuit St George.

> *The* WAITER *exits.*

You remember it?

EDITH: No.

JOHN: We drank it at the Hotel de la Paix in Geneva on my first night there with the Australian delegation. I thought it the finest thing I had ever drunk. You chose it. By then you were a connoisseur of all things French.

EDITH: I'm touched that you remember.

> *The* WAITER *enters and pours the wine. Then exits. They clink glasses and drink.*

JOHN: Here's to my incisiveness and relentless logic once again over-powering you.

EDITH: I'm sensing that you are now impatient with me.

JOHN: Not at all.

EDITH: Perhaps you are no longer in need of a candid friend?

JOHN: Perhaps I have become aware of what might be driving the candour.

EDITH: What do you mean?

JOHN: The lack of an otherwise sphere of influence.

EDITH: You think I lack influence?

JOHN: I think it. I know it. You know it.

EDITH: And if I do?
JOHN: You do.

Pause.

EDITH: Why would you say that to me?
JOHN: Because in combination with your lavender marriage, I'm worried about you.
EDITH: Not worried that you'll hurt me.
JOHN: Worried that you'll fall back on physical charms that have always been your most reliable asset.
EDITH: I'm not quite sure, but did you just call me a tramp?
JOHN: Can you say no?
EDITH: Of course I can.
JOHN: Always?
EDITH: Yes, always.
JOHN: But there have been grey areas.
EDITH: For everyone.
JOHN: No, Edith, if you're not anyone's then you can be anyone's. People sense it and they take the opportunity. Have you never wondered?
EDITH: I thought people just found me irresistible.
JOHN: Yes, and that's one power you can rely on. But the more Ambrose shows his colours the more vulnerable you'll be.
EDITH: I think this is just conservative prudery dressed up as candour.
JOHN: Is it?
EDITH: Or perhaps it's just that I've never given you the opportunity.
JOHN: I was your father's friend.
EDITH: As if that makes any difference.

Pause.

JOHN: A protégée will in most cases be overwhelmed and submit to the superior mind. Such a submission is honourable and no pride is lost.
EDITH: Then perhaps I can no longer be a protégée.
JOHN: And perhaps that is what I'm sensing.
EDITH: In fact, I am now opposing you outright. On matters of serious principle and intellectual substance. Even on experience. We are now in conflict.

A meal is put before them.

JOHN: I refused to sign The Call to the People of Australia.

EDITH: Why was that?

JOHN: It wasn't because I was unpatriotic. It was just that the wording of the call was too clerical. I don't think the Australian people need finger-wagging warnings by church leaders and judges such as me against alien philosophies 'which sap the will and darken the understanding and breed evil dissentions'.

EDITH: I hear that the chief justices of all the states signed it. And all the church leaders. All the bigwigs.

JOHN: You know what is frightening them?

EDITH: I thought it was just fear that Australia will become socialist and atheist?

JOHN: Oh, that too, but what really frightens them is that the women who worked while their men were at war won't go back to the home. They fear working women will find earning a wage more interesting than marriage. The Call is for women to stop working and stay at home.

EDITH: Maybe women could learn to work *and* raise children.

JOHN: I was the only judge who didn't sign. I'm surprised you know about The Call. It's not being launched until later this year.

EDITH: We hear things ahead of time in Canberra.

Pause.

Before I leave …

JOHN: You're going then?

EDITH: Yes.

JOHN: Yes.

EDITH: Thank you for going to my father's funeral.

JOHN: Not at all.

EDITH: Did you give the oration?

JOHN: No, a local chap gave it. As the local mayor, he thought he out-ranked me.

EDITH: George McDowell. He's an old friend of the family.

EDITH *stands.*

Goodbye, John.

JOHN: Goodnight, Edith. *Salus populi suprema est lex.* The safety of the people is the supreme law.

EDITH: *Et propter vitam vivendi perdere causas.* We surrender precious freedoms on the pretence of protecting them.

JOHN: I simply argued that it is Parliament who should determine when there is an enemy in our midst. Not the courts.

EDITH: And when that Parliament uses malign claims about the seriousness of a crisis to cause panic and persecute one's legitimate opponents?

JOHN: The Constitution does not mean to create perilous delays in the ability of a government to determine whether we are facing a crisis.

EDITH: We are not at war with the communists within Australia.

JOHN: We do not have to wait for the bullets to fly.

> JOHN *slugs down the last of his drink and exits.*

> EDITH *recites from 'The Rhyme of Joyous Garde':*

EDITH: And now she is dead, men tell me, and I,
    In   this   living   death   must   I   linger   and   lie

> Till my cup to the dregs is drunken?
> I looked through the lattice, worn and grim,
> With eyelids darken'd and eyesight dim,
> And weary body and wasted limb,
>   And sinew slacken'd and shrunken.

The lights fade.

END OF ACT ONE

ACT TWO

SCENE TEN: THE RADICALISM OF ITS TIME

Berry cemetery. There are two seashell-covered graves on stage. GEORGE MCDOWELL *stands next to them, dressed in a dark suit with brown shoes and an elaborate mayoral chain.*

EDITH, JANICE *and* FRED *enter.*

EDITH: George. This is my brother Frederick and his friend Miss Linnett.

JANICE: Janice.

EDITH: This is George McDowell who is the local mayor and who gave the eulogy at our father's funeral.

GEORGE: Call me T. George. Everyone does.

FRED: Like T. rex.

GEORGE: What's that?

FRED: Nothing. A dinosaur fossil. Please go on, George.

GEORGE: T. George.

    Beat.

You will see they are in the Old Section. They shouldn't be there but there was nowhere else.

EDITH: No rationalist section.

GEORGE: No. And there weren't a lot of epitaphs that the mason could do. Your father chose 'At rest—life's journey o'er' for your mother so we did that for your father too. He had wanted a longer statement but it wouldn't fit and the mason thought it might be controversial.

FRED: And we can't have that in the Berry cemetery.

GEORGE: I couldn't find an order of service to be held for relatives visiting a burial site so long after the burial.

EDITH: It never crossed my mind that there would be.

GEORGE: So I worked one up myself.

    EDITH *looks at* JANICE.

JANICE: Let's have a glass of wine before we begin.

    JANICE *goes to a picnic basket and pours wine for all of them.*

GEORGE *takes a small felt-covered box and places it next to the graves. He looks up at the sky.*

GEORGE: We have assembled to bid a kind and solemn farewell to our dear friends and mother and father of Edith Alison Campbell Berry and Frederick David Campbell Berry.

Cecelia Gladys Thomas, a rationalist and reform organiser was born on 17 March 1880 at Albury, New South Wales. Her father was a sheriff's officer and her mother was the great-granddaughter of Governor King. As a young woman she visited the prisons with her father. The family moved to Melbourne and she studied Charles Darwin, Thomas Paine and Edward Bellamy with a tutor at home. She attempted an elopement with the tutor at the age of fifteen which did not last more than a month or so …

EDITH: What? [*Laughing*] I've never heard this. Did you know this?

FRED: [*also suppressing laughter*] No.

GEORGE: You are not worried by this information? You shouldn't be. It is a rather poetic act of passion, I would've thought, for a young person. Romeo and Juliet.

EDITH: Depends on the age of the tutor.

FRED *now laughs out loud.*

GEORGE *frowns but continues.*

GEORGE: She had a fine contralto voice and she performed with the Metropolitan Lieder …

He struggles.

EDITH & FRED: [*in unison*] *Liedertafel.*

GEORGE: She told me that to pay for her musical training she started a poultry farm at Deepdene, building the poultry sheds from scrap timber. By 1900 she was a poultry expert as well as a teacher of singing and voice production.

EDITH *and* FRED *are still laughing and now* JANICE *joins them.*

As you both remember, your mother refused to wear a wedding ring on the grounds that it symbolised servitude to a spouse. She had this stated during her rationalist wedding to Peter Berry.

JANICE: Good for her.

GEORGE: The couple moved to the country at Jaspers Brush and with two others formed the Children's Peace Army. On one occasion, at a celebration of the Russian Revolution when unionists insisted on displaying the red flag prohibited by the War Precautions Act, your mother enlisted the children in the Peace Army to pull down a large man and with one foot on his chest your mother tied a red ribbon around his neck.

FRED: Where is she now when we need her to do that to Menzies?

GEORGE: It is generally agreed that she dressed very well, often in beautifully tailored suits, sometimes with brass buttons carrying her initials.

FRED: I don't remember initialled buttons.

EDITH: They didn't last long. And you had disappeared by then.

GEORGE: Never robust, she died of liver cirrhosis.

EDITH: I thought it was cancer.

FRED: I just never knew.

Pause.

EDITH: She insisted that I not come home for the funeral.

FRED: No, of course not.

GEORGE: I'm not sure I understand.

EDITH: I was working with the League of Nations.

FRED: And in her mind that was the universal cause of the day, and a cause takes precedence over family. That's why they were always away. I would sit, scared stiff in that big house, and I would strap on my sheath knife for protection from the dark. They'd come home late, smelling of drink.

EDITH: I would wake when I heard the car and go down to them. I remember watching her undress and prepare for bed.

FRED: I never went into her bedroom.

EDITH: No, you never demanded the intimacy with her that I did. However slight and desperate a thread it was.

They both take deep draughts of the wine.

JANICE: God, I hope people will be able to record such radical achievements for me.

FRED: It was, I suppose, the radicalism of its time. They had no real training in theory.

EDITH: Go on, T. George. Do father now.

FRED: An abbreviated version, if you please.

GEORGE: But this is the one I actually wrote.

EDITH: I'd like to hear it.

GEORGE: I'd always assumed, when you disappeared from their lives, that there'd been a breach.

FRED: That's right.

GEORGE: Will you say what it was?

FRED: They left home years before I did.

GEORGE: If you care to listen to the eulogy you'll understand what he was doing. He applied his intelligence to the study of water. Drilling methods, types of piping, tanking, sterilising. He invented and patented a special no-leak tap for water tanks which should have been taken up by every home and council in the country, but never was. He believed in cheap uncensored mail and free uncensored libraries and he believed that political pamphlets should be distributed free of charge through the post. He left a trunk full of manuscripts, including his first pamphlet after reading Law titled 'Our Financiers, Their Ignorance, Usurpations and Frauds'.

JANICE: You had wonderful parents.

FRED: Thank you, Janice. They were just tinkering with injustice.

EDITH: Fuck.

> *The others look at her in surprise.*

This is all too morbid, too hot, I want to go to a cool hotel lounge. With no flies. But first I want to do this. Fred.

> *She hands* FRED *her own wine glass and then fills both his and hers with wine.*

> *She goes over to the graves and pours one glass on each.*

They always enjoyed wine.

GEORGE: Following your grandfather's death, your mother inherited his significant shareholding in a major Hunter Valley vineyard.

EDITH: Then I am not being entirely inappropriate.

JANICE: It doesn't matter if you are.

> *Beat.*

I'll take these to the car.

GEORGE: This was, I imagine, a rather demanding visit.

> *He takes* EDITH's *hand.* JANICE *exits, carrying the glasses.*

If you would like to hear the full eulogy I can come and see you. I could drive to Canberra.

EDITH: I don't think so, George. But thank you for today.

GEORGE: Candid, pure, serene, noble and yet for years he was maligned and slandered, simply because he had a forthright nature.

GEORGE *exits.*

EDITH: I have never in my life said that word aloud before. And I would never, ever say it in front of my mother and father.

FRED: Don't worry. I don't think they were listening.

Pause.

EDITH: I have not helped anyone to find water.

FRED *puts his hand on her shoulder.*

FRED: Nor have I.

SCENE ELEVEN: BLOOMSBURY ON THE MOLONGLO

Edith and Ambrose's home in Arthur Circle, Forrest.

EDITH *recites from 'The Rhyme of Joyous Garde':*

EDITH: Through the lattice rushes the south wind, dense
    With fumes of the flowery frankincense
      From hawthorn blossoming thickly;
    And gold is shower'd on grass unshorn,
    And poppy-fire on shuddering corn,
    With May-dew flooded and flush'd with morn,
      And scented with sweetness sickly.

AMELIA RICHTER *enters, carrying an* apfelstrudel.

Amelia.

AMELIA: I didn't mean to scare you.

AMBROSE *enters.*

EDITH: No, no, come in.

AMELIA: I saw the lights on and I thought I'd poke my head in.

EDITH: Ambrose, look who's here. Our somewhat Bloomsbury new friend Amelia. The Dane.

AMBROSE: Then I expect those are Danish pastries, are they, Amelia?

AMELIA: It is an *apfelstrudel* because I know how much you both like it.

AMBROSE: *Apfelstrudel* is a sure giveaway, Miss Denmark, that you are in fact German.

AMELIA: We only posed as Danish when we arrived after the war. We would never have got accommodation otherwise.

EDITH: Come in. Sit down. What other scandalous activities have you been undertaking apart from baking *apfelstrudel*?

AMELIA: I might be hard-pressed to provide scandal, Edith. Oh no, I do have something. I ordered the *Kinsey Report* from Sydney.

AMBROSE: And what do you make of it?

AMELIA: Well, the statistics about how many sexual partners people have in their life shocked me. It's a lot more than you would think. A lot more than I've had.

EDITH: And is that why you've come bearing *apfelstrudel*? Looking to increase your statistics?

AMELIA: Edith! Don't make brazen suggestions you're not prepared to put into practice.

EDITH: How do you know that I'm not?

AMELIA: You're both positively indecent.

AMBROSE: Just what we were discussing before you arrived.

AMELIA: What were you discussing?

AMBROSE: I want to do a song and dance act for the Legacy concert. Edith vetoed it.

AMELIA: No. But why?

EDITH: Ambrose wanted to do it with his friend from the Commonwealth office, Allen. *En femme*.

AMELIA: You mean …?

AMBROSE: It was to be a burlesque. A decadent Berlin burlesque.

AMELIA: And would you be …?

AMBROSE: In persona feminine, my dear? In full wig and gown and lipstick? Well, yes.

    Pause.

EDITH: The idea is too outrageous for Legacy, especially in Canberra. Don't you encourage him, Amelia.

AMELIA: It would certainly liven things up. Help push Canberra into maturity as a city. We never see anything like that here.

EDITH: And is that what you Germans call not encouraging someone?

AMELIA: Well, if he doesn't do it for Legacy he should do it for us, here.

AMBROSE: Would you really like to see it?

EDITH: Ambrose, no. Really—it's far too late.

AMELIA: But I've just arrived and it's Friday night after all.

EDITH: No.

AMELIA: Ambrose, please, let me see.

EDITH: It'll take too long. Getting dressed and all. It is *en femme* after all.

AMBROSE: I could just wear something from your wardrobe.

Pause.

EDITH: Now my advice is ignored even in my own home.

AMELIA: But he needs to do it in honour of Dr Kinsey. Surely.

EDITH *waves her hand in permission.*

EDITH: Go on then. But don't take too long or we will lose interest.

AMBROSE *exits, excitedly.*

You shouldn't have encouraged him.

AMELIA: We'll turn out the lights. Now. What can we use for a spotlight? How about this table lamp, it's got a lovely flexible neck. That'll turn upwards like so.

She manoeuvres the lamp into position.

Perfect. Now. A suitable song. What have you got?

EDITH: Cole Porter. *Kiss Me Kate.*

AMELIA: This is the most fun I've had since I came to Canberra.

EDITH: Please don't encourage him to do it for the Legacy concert.

AMELIA: But why? Every decent city has a Weimar colour. They were done in every prisoner of war camp during the war.

EDITH: So we have a German, posing as a Dane, telling Legacy that this sort of thing is alright because it was done in the camps?

AMELIA: Well, you're the ones with the light, and the song.

EDITH: And the wig.

AMELIA: Really?

EDITH: Really.

AMELIA: Have you visited Karmel's and seen their collection of erotic art?

EDITH: No.

AMELIA: You must. It's rather, well, educational. And that's in Canberra. I'm sure it would be fine to do it for a fundraiser.

EDITH *puts on the music to 'Why Can't You Behave?'*

AMBROSE makes his entrance and mimes to the Ella Fitzgerald version of 'Why Can't You Behave?'. He finishes with a flourish towards AMELIA. She squeals in delight.

Bravo.

AMBROSE: Really?

AMELIA: You're so convincing.

AMBROSE: And so fetching.

AMELIA: Absolutely.

EDITH: Positively gorgeous, darling.

AMELIA: And every inch the Weimar girl. You must do it for Legacy.

AMBROSE: Then I think I need a flapper dress from the twenties—more beads and tassels and slinkiness.

AMELIA laughs again. AMBROSE takes EDITH's chin in his hands.

Can I?

EDITH: No.

AMBROSE: Really?

EDITH: No.

AMBROSE: But what are you afraid of?

EDITH: A catastrophe.

AMBROSE: We're living in a shell here, Edith. I'm suffocating.

He accompanies this plea with elaborate hand gestures and fluttering eyelashes.

EDITH: Oh, alright. Where's the fun in being starchy?

AMBROSE: Thank you, dear Edith.

EDITH: I'm glad for you.

He goes to kiss her. At first she turns away. Then almost reluctantly she turns back and he kisses her, more perfunctorily than he would have. EDITH pulls away and smiles at AMELIA. AMELIA and AMBROSE exit.

SCENE TWELVE: SPINNING THE WORLD ON ONE'S THUMB

Edith's office.

GIBSON *enters.*

GIBSON: Sir George Pepler told me that was the best organised Town Planning conference he had ever been to.

EDITH: I'm pleased.

GIBSON: Insisting that the hotels offer rugs and blankets that delegates could bring along to the conference was a master stroke.

EDITH: Well, the power restrictions were as a result of the communist-led miners stopping work one day a week.

GIBSON: Not that you're to blame for that. Your brother, maybe.

EDITH: The blankets didn't stop the delegates abandoning the east lake.

GIBSON: No.

EDITH: Even though it is in Griffin's original plan.

GIBSON: I heard you telling Sir George that in conversation. In fact, I'm sure I heard the words 'You cannot have too many lakes in Australia because we yearn for expanses of water'.

EDITH: I did say that. I also argued that it would bring moisture to the air and that a lake intrigues people, suggesting that there is something of interest to be seen on the other side.

GIBSON: And how did that play with Old Man Pepler?

EDITH: He told me that the way to keep warm in Canberra is to fill your bicycle handlebars with warm water before you set out.

GIBSON: Right.

EDITH: You're laughing at me.

GIBSON: Not at all.

EDITH: I meant what I said about Griffin's original plan being respected.

GIBSON: There is a grand manner to the plans which I dislike.

EDITH: You say grand manner, I say distinctiveness.

GIBSON: That's what you say about the width of the streets.

EDITH: If you reduce them as you plan to do they will lack distinction.

GIBSON: They will only lack the potential for more accidents than any other Australian city.

EDITH: Then people should stop their cars and study their maps.

GIBSON: I don't think so.

EDITH: They will. The streets will tell them that they are in the capital.

GIBSON: Capital.

EDITH: But this is not any old town, it is the capital.

GIBSON: Then you should keep saying so. Not that anyone will notice.

EDITH: I will.

GIBSON: Just like a schoolchild with a new subject.

EDITH: That's cruel.

GIBSON: Then don't say capital.

EDITH: Why not?

GIBSON: I don't know. Maybe just to have one less thing that you argue with me against.

EDITH: So why do you keep me on?

GIBSON: You're efficient.

EDITH: Is that all?

GIBSON: That's quite a lot.

EDITH: Not really.

GIBSON: Do you want to stay on as my dogsbody or not?

> EDITH *nods, biting her lip.*
>
> *She struggles not to cry.*
>
> *She takes out a compact and carefully fixes her face in the compact mirror.*

SCENE THIRTEEN: DECLARATION OF THE FREE

EDITH *and* RICHARD *are at The Commonwealth Club.*

RICHARD: You don't think I behaved like a reprobate on that night of the dinner? I couldn't believe I did what I did.

EDITH: I couldn't believe I let you, Richard.

RICHARD: Comes from your being so long in Europe.

EDITH: And at a PM's dinner.

RICHARD: That's right.

> *Beat.*

I mean … I don't mean to imply anything when I say European. You know what I mean.

EDITH: I'm taking it as a compliment.

RICHARD: I suppose if anyone had observed it they wouldn't have believed their eyes. You don't think anyone did, do you?

EDITH: I told my husband about it later, but not at the dinner, no. Indeed, I had a very productive conversation with Gibson, the city planner, who I now work with at Interior.

RICHARD: I know. I kept track of you but could do nothing … about you.

> *He puts out his hand and holds hers. She allows it and then pulls away.*

EDITH: So.
RICHARD: So.
EDITH: Are you recovered from the accident?
RICHARD: I'm fine.

> *Beat.*

The children are making sense, in their own way of something that has no sense. They're with their grandparents in Sydney. The injuries were minor but that's part of the challenge. We all escaped with minor injuries while their mother was killed. Same accident. And we escaped.

EDITH: You must think me callous, getting in touch now.

> *Pause.*

RICHARD: I think we sometimes display conventional feelings as a way of reflecting the expectations of the person bearing condolences.
EDITH: I don't think our encounters can be described as conventional.
RICHARD: No.
EDITH: In which case, where shall we go?

> *He looks at her, flushed.*

RICHARD: Should we eat lunch, for appearances?
EDITH: I don't think I could eat lunch.
RICHARD: We could go to my house.
EDITH: How would that feel for you?
RICHARD: As insensitive as it sounds, I don't think it really matters. Maybe she would be happy for me. And the dead are blind.
EDITH: So they are.
RICHARD: Shall we go?
EDITH: Tell me about her bedroom.
RICHARD: It is very feminine, pink and grey with lace-edged pillow covers.
EDITH: Have you still been sleeping in there?
RICHARD: Not since she died.
EDITH: But that is where you will take me?
RICHARD: Yes.
EDITH: How?
RICHARD: I will roll down your stockings and push off your corset and pull down your silk panties.

EDITH: No teasing of the moment?

RICHARD: No need. You're wet already. So I will thrust myself into you in one easy movement, filling you, hard.

EDITH: And then?

RICHARD: Then I will wrap you in my dead wife's kimono and with my semen running down your legs onto it I will take you again on the lounge room floor.

EDITH: And what will I say?

RICHARD: Give me a child.

Pause.

EDITH: I have never said that. I have never been pregnant.

RICHARD: Then you will know the unique charge of saying it. Aloud.

EDITH: The entire proposal is utter perversity.

RICHARD: Interested?

Pause.

EDITH: I'll be at your place. In an hour.

RICHARD *exits.* AMBROSE *appears.*

I need to tell you about the knee-touching man.

AMBROSE: Oh. He's resurfaced then?

EDITH: Actually I contacted him.

AMBROSE: I see.

EDITH: I'm going to him now.

AMBROSE: Have fun. Take notes.

EDITH: This is not for one night.

AMBROSE: How can you know?

EDITH: I know.

AMBROSE: You can't know.

Pause.

EDITH: We always said that the rule was to be home before morning.

AMBROSE: We did.

EDITH: But this … is going to be different.

Pause.

AMBROSE: Had enough of this old nancy-boy?

EDITH: No. Not like that.

AMBROSE: Wait. See how this turns out. We should wait on the turn of
    events, should we not?

EDITH: I know how it will turn out.

AMBROSE: How so?

EDITH: One knows.

AMBROSE: When one can try to be a proper woman with a proper man.

EDITH: Maybe.

AMBROSE: Except of course that you are a crooked woman.

EDITH: Who needs only a little straightening out.

    Pause.

AMBROSE: I'll await your return, then. Titillation can sometimes lead us
    to stray too far. Worth doing, though. I applaud.

EDITH: I'll go now. Try to be stout about it.

AMBROSE: Have you consulted our *Book of Crossroads*?

EDITH: I'm not reading that particular book anymore.

AMBROSE: I'll let you go now.

    AMBROSE *stands on stage.*

    The lights change. EDITH *straddles* RICHARD *and begins to move
    on him in a sexually provocative way.*

RICHARD: Don't like the bed?

EDITH: Don't need the bed.

RICHARD: Like being on top?

EDITH: Like this position.

RICHARD: Why is that?

EDITH: It gives me the strange physical sensation that the penis is mine
    and I am in fact thrusting it into you.

RICHARD: Does it now?

EDITH: It does.

    She thrusts on top of him.

Doesn't it?

RICHARD: Yes.

EDITH: Yes.

    They continue taking pleasure in each other.

SCENE FOURTEEN: MY BROTHER'S KEEPER

AMBROSE *performs a silent burlesque, or a reprieve of 'Why Can't You Behave?' as* RICHARD *and* EDITH *continue to make love on the other side of the stage.*

Suddenly, in a choreographed act of violence, two MEN *set upon* AMBROSE *and bloody his nose.*

EDITH *finishes with* RICHARD *and goes to* AMBROSE. *She holds his head back but the blood is going everywhere.*

EDITH: What happened?

AMBROSE: Apparently I'm a disgrace to manhood.

EDITH: You went into the men's toilets to change?

AMBROSE: There's always a queue in the ladies'.

> *Beat.*

What, no laugh?

EDITH: Did you say something to one of them?

AMBROSE: I may have nodded and smiled. Or winked. I definitely didn't blow him a kiss.

EDITH: Stop it.

AMBROSE: You might at least have said that blood-red suits me. Though I'd far rather stick to the nails than the nose.

EDITH: At least the High Commissioner didn't see you.

> AMBROSE *is silent.*

You're joking?

AMBROSE: I used my real name in the printed program so he wouldn't fail to recognise me.

> *Pause.*

What, no more approbation? You were the one who wanted me not to do it.

EDITH: I was wrong. You're a brave, brave girl. And beautiful.

> AMBROSE *closes his eyes for a kiss. But* EDITH *turns away.*

AMBROSE: So your public servant. It's been going on since the PM's dinner?

EDITH: No, I sent him a condolence card about the death of his wife.

AMBROSE: Well, I was going to say I was disappointed that there was no deceit or betrayal, but it's just that it's not of me.

EDITH: No, not of you.

AMBROSE: I called over his file.

EDITH: Is he a good man?

AMBROSE: As good as the public service might want. If you were a person who wanted a good man.

EDITH: I thought I might try it for a change.

> *Pause.*

But please do tell me if anything truly awful about him comes across your desk.

AMBROSE: I can't do that, Edith.

EDITH: Why not?

AMBROSE: The HC says that he'll see me recalled.

EDITH: Recalled?

AMBROSE: He was on his way into the toilets when I was on my way out. Only stopped to land his own punch. Dress too short, act too long, nose too bloody.

> *Pause.*

EDITH: Do you think that your secret life—our secret life—will come out and be talked about?

AMBROSE: Worried that I might diminish the dazzle of your erotic affair of the heart? The wife of a disgraced diplomat who deserts her husband at his time of need. The humiliation of being relegated to a socially embarrassing aberration. And what if the gossip should reach your all-male lover? Or harm his career? Oh, the disreputable ambiguity of your past liaison with such a person.

EDITH: It is reasonable to be concerned.

AMBROSE: If being a pansy were an offence in the Foreign Office they would be seriously short-staffed. I think the discomfort of a few scandalised churchmen is all that was considered.

EDITH: When you perform, people can see more than that. You reveal something about yourself. And therefore about us. About me.

AMBROSE: Then you'd best go be a proper wife to a proper man with all its conventions. I do hope he has grieving children.

EDITH: Two.

AMBROSE: Then you can play the understanding stepmother. That's sure to quell any gossip left over from me.

Pause.

EDITH: I suggest that for the time being we say that I am staying back here to clean things up. That I intend to follow.

AMBROSE: Which you could do. When you're finished your *amourette*. You could skip back to London. We'll be happier there. More hijinx there.

EDITH: I think I've now made my bed here. I hope. What is happening is very serious.

AMBROSE: A last-gasp attempt to really fit in.

EDITH: If you see it like that.

AMBROSE: Watch out for Fred and Janice. I can't see them suiting this new picture.

EDITH: I am not my brother's keeper.

Pause.

AMBROSE: Aren't you? I found the communist papers in the tack room.

EDITH: You found the papers?

AMBROSE: Yes.

EDITH: But what did you think?

AMBROSE: I thought you had put me at risk and you wouldn't mind if I indulged in a little of my own skulduggery.

EDITH: Do you think this has anything to do with …?

AMBROSE: No. I sent some of it in my dispatches. Not much there of interest, but I included it anyway.

EDITH: You always wanted to go back to London.

AMBROSE: Perhaps.

Pause.

EDITH: When will the recall take effect?

AMBROSE: It was to be immediately, but just today I've heard of a hitch. There's a fellow at the Soviet embassy claims there's a spy ring in Australia. Vladimir Petrov, we met him socially.

EDITH: And what do they want you to do?

AMBROSE: There'll be Royal Commission hearings for a while. Not that they know anything like as much as British Intelligence. But then we know more about the Communist Party than they know themselves. Then there'll be a farewell garden party at the HC, I imagine.

EDITH: So, until you go, you'll stay here?

AMBROSE: If you want to avoid tricky questions. And I know that you do.

> EDITH *wets her wedding finger with saliva. She takes off her wedding ring and puts it on* AMBROSE.

EDITH: Be married to us both. For our old selves. That way our old selves will always be married.

AMBROSE: Yes, always married. You and me. The two of me. The three of us.

SCENE FIFTEEN: MOUNT BLEAKNESS IN THE GARDEN

EISENHOWER: [*voice-over*] To pause there would be to confirm the hopeless finality that two atomic colossi are doomed malevolently to eye each other indefinitely across a trembling world. To stop there would be to accept helplessly the probability of civilisation destroyed, the annihilation of the irreplaceable heritage of mankind handed down to us from generation to generation, and the condemnation of mankind to begin all over again the age-old struggle upward from savagery toward decency, and right, and justice. Surely no sane member of the human race could discover victory in such desolation. Could anyone wish his name to be coupled by history with such human degradation and destruction?

> *Richard's home.*

> EDITH *enters, excitedly.*

EDITH: They've accepted it.

RICHARD: What?

EDITH: It's the most substantial thing I've done since I've returned to Australia.

RICHARD: Are you talking about the *ANZAAS Journal*?

EDITH: 'Atoms for Peace and the Future of Specialised Diplomacy' by Edith Campbell Berry, Bachelor of Science, Syd.

RICHARD: They're publishing it?

EDITH: Thank you for your help.

RICHARD: I just tweaked the science.

EDITH: Eisenhower is calling for an International Atomic Energy Agency. It will be a small League of Nations. And that's the future, don't you see? Specialised organisations will solve one problem at a time instead of one organisation trying to solve all the world's problems. And with this, I·position myself to be noticed.

RICHARD: Nuclear power is the future.

EDITH: And now I'm on the winning team.

RICHARD: We are the future.

He dips her backwards and kisses her.

EDITH: Seriously, Richard. Menzies can't stop talking about making Australia a uranium power among nations. That way he's in on the secrets, seated at the table with the Americans.

RICHARD: You should turn it into a book.

EDITH: Do you think?

RICHARD: The government will fund it, and if they do, I'll bet the Education Department will distribute it.

EDITH: I'll have to resign from Gibson's office.

RICHARD: Then it's just as well I've asked Menzies to find you something in the Australian Atomic Energy Commission.

Pause.

EDITH: How?

RICHARD: I might have had him read a little something.

EDITH: Did you show him my paper?

RICHARD: I showed him a summary.

EDITH: What did he say?

RICHARD: He said he wants you inside the tent. To explain it all to him.

EDITH: Really? He said 'inside the tent'?

RICHARD: Public Liaison Advisor.

EDITH: Oh, Richard.

RICHARD: You'll have an office in the Prime Minister's corridor.

EDITH: In Parliament House?

RICHARD: There's no salary, but they'll give you travelling expenses and a per diem.

EDITH: No salary?

Beat.

I suppose it's a start.

RICHARD: It really is.

EDITH: You told him about my time at the League and UN double-R A?

RICHARD: Actually what seemed to seal the deal was your still being on the invitation list at the British High Commission.

EDITH: I see.

RICHARD: He's providing the British with any test sites they want for the bombs.

EDITH: Oh yes, he loves to talk about preserving our ancient structural unity.

RICHARD: What?

EDITH: Nothing.

RICHARD: You can stop playing the innocent, you know.

EDITH: Sorry?

RICHARD: I know you were working for the British Secret Service through your ex-husband.

EDITH: Was I?

RICHARD: And using your brother as a way of getting to know things. People say you were responsible for getting the names of those CSIRO scientist members of the Party for ASIO.

EDITH: Do they?

RICHARD: I don't expect you to tell me outright, but you can stop pretending a weary intolerance for the Brits.

EDITH: I think I may have to minimise my contact with Fred and Janice even further.

RICHARD: You know I had you checked before we went too far as a couple?

EDITH: I didn't have you checked.

RICHARD: Well, you didn't have to. I'm a public servant.

EDITH: Good character and political neutrality?

RICHARD: There was evidently much laughter too when the man from ASIO was sent to interview you. He was the laughing stock of the agency I'm told, because he failed to determine whether you were a British agent, which was the intention of the interview. It was a joke played on the guy that they sent. A training exercise.

EDITH: I see.

Beat.

So this new position is not really down to your influence, my darling, but because I'm a woman shrouded in mystery?

RICHARD: It'll be a blurry role in any case. You write well in everyday language, that's what Menzies liked about your essay. So you're perfect to be his interpreter of the screeds of stuff the AAEC sends.

EDITH: The management of low expectations, then?

RICHARD: Come on, let's go to the Gloucester to celebrate. At least it gets you out of planning.

EDITH: True.

Beat.

Richard.

RICHARD: What?

EDITH: Something else happened today. With the children.

RICHARD: Oh, that's right, there was no school for the boys today, was there?

EDITH: No, and I didn't go into work. Deliberately, to spend time with them.

RICHARD: They'll get used to you.

EDITH: Of course they will.

RICHARD: I know that they only look at me during breakfast. I'm sure that will change.

EDITH: They walked in on me when I was having a bath.

RICHARD: Right.

EDITH: My first reaction, which I regret, was to shout at them and tell them to get out.

RICHARD: Why didn't you lock the door?

EDITH: I'm not ashamed of my body and I'm not planning to pass embarrassment about the human body on to the boys.

RICHARD: I'm sorry. I'll tell them to knock.

EDITH: No, I wrapped myself in a towel and I went and found them. I told them that we should not be ashamed of our nakedness. Most of all we should not be ashamed of our curiosity about life. Then I let them have a look.

RICHARD: At what?

EDITH: At my body.

RICHARD: You did what?

EDITH: I explained my breasts. I showed them my nipples. I showed them that I have no penis and I told them that my vagina was inside my pubic hair.

RICHARD: What were they doing during this … anatomy lesson?

EDITH: They asked me why boys have nipples—which you have to admit is a highly intelligent response. I was quite devastated not to have an adequate answer for them. I mumbled something about being left over in our evolutionary progress, and then I told them to go outside and play. It's a pity, don't you think?

RICHARD: What, exactly?

EDITH: Not to have an answer to their first serious question of me as their stepmother.

RICHARD: I think they'll live.

Beat.

In fact I think this raises something I've been meaning to broach for a while.

EDITH: Mmm?

RICHARD: I think it's time the boys went to my old school, to King's, to board.

EDITH: You think I did the wrong thing?

RICHARD: I think you are more fearful of prudery than I am.

EDITH: I see.

RICHARD: My family has a long history of embarrassment about the human body. Who am I to question it?

EDITH: Don't you mean who are we?

Pause.

RICHARD: Of all the things that require change, parenting is not one of them.

EDITH: I can't agree with that.

RICHARD: As a compromise, let's just teach them to knock, shall we?

EDITH: Of course.

RICHARD *exits.*

SCENE SIXTEEN: NO LONGER A DELIBERATE MAN

The ensemble drunkenly sing 'The Ballad of Eureka', an Australian protest song inspired by the Eureka Rebellion of 1854.

ALL: [*singing*] There's not a flag in Europe
        More lovely to behold,
        Than floats above Eureka
        Where diggers work the gold.

        There's not a flag in Europe
        More lovely to the eye,
        Than is the blue and silver
        Against a southern sky.

        Here in the name of freedom,
        Whatever be our loss,
        We swear to stand together
        Beneath the Southern Cross.

University House, Acton.

Three COMMUNIST PARTY GOERS *enter, with balloons and streamers, accompanied by* JANICE *and* FRED.

The PARTY GOERS *proceed to pour themselves drinks.*

FRED: I've suggested not drinking until after the Party business.

EDITH: Well I, dear brother, am with the ill-disciplined, I'm afraid. Let them fortify themselves for the news ahead.

FRED: That the whole history of the Soviet Union has been a barbarous lie and a disaster.

JANICE: There's only a half-gallon flagon.

EDITH: Which is perfectly acceptable as a *vin ordinaire*.

JANICE: I wasn't expecting you, Edith, or I would have brought more.

EDITH: Well, it's history in the making, isn't it, this letter from Khrushchev? You didn't believe me when Ambrose first sent it via his diplomatic bag.

FRED: I remember saying that it was the cleverest piece of propaganda since the war.

    Beat.

If only it was.

JANICE: At least the wine makes the cover story about a birthday party slightly more convincing.

EDITH: You don't think that a few balloons and streamers will fool ASIO.

JANICE: It's not for ASIO. It's for the Central Committee in Sydney, they haven't sanctioned the discussion of Khrushchev's revelations.

FRED *taps his bottle with a spoon.*

FRED: It's time we started business. I'd just like to begin by reminding you that this is not a branch meeting or a cadre meeting. It's an exchange of ideas among comrades. Something that has only been condoned because, well, Canberra is different.

PARTY GOER 1: Let's start with the Soviet invasion of Hungary?

FRED: We are here to discuss Khrushchev's speech at the Congress.

PARTY GOER 2: Answer the question.

JANICE: The Soviet has come to the aid of an allied communist state where the Americans are fomenting unrest.

PARTY GOER 3: Bullshit.

JANICE: Let's keep the discussion orderly, shall we?

PARTY GOER 1: What's orderly about Khrushchev's claims? Stalin putting thousands of Party members up on counter-revolutionary claims, thousands arrested and shot, tens of thousands declared enemies of the people.

PARTY GOER 2: Had Postyshev killed because he called himself a Bolshevik.

PARTY GOER 3: So now criticism is insolence?

PARTY GOER 1: And insolence gets you shot?

FRED: In the wrong time and place, yes.

JANICE: The important thing is the correct handling of this within the interests of the Party. Which does not mean endless debate at all levels of the Party. We do not want to go back to the 1920s and argue all those matters that were resolved then about the dangers of factions and the need for Party discipline. The leadership has acknowledged the problem of the cult of the individual.

PARTY GOER 2: And continue to practise it.

PARTY GOER 1: All those statues of Stalin and busts and photographs in every shop. Street names changed, songs written about him and on and on. He was a dictator and according to Khrushchev he was a butcher.

JANICE: The Party structure is the only way of formulating policy. It can't come from drunken discussions in pubs by university students who think they know everything.

There is a drunken jeer.

PARTY GOER 3: We're losing members and do not really have a correct line from the leadership. There's indecision. Tactically, the leadership should not have shown surprise when the truth about Stalin's murderous and barbaric actions came out.

JANICE: Stalinism was the cleansing of the Party.

PARTY GOER 1: He had loyal Party members accused and murdered.

FRED: The Russian Revolution is the greatest achievement of the International Working Class and must be preserved at all costs.

But the jeering resumes and smashing of bottles begins.

JANICE: Declare the meeting closed.

FRED: I declare the formal part of this meeting closed.

PARTY GOER 2 starts singing the chorus of the satirical Tom Lehrer song 'We Will All Go Together When We Go':

As they exit, the others join him in the song, drinking and jeering.

FRED sinks into a chair.

JANICE: I knew calling this meeting was an error. A serious error.

EDITH: They'll be too drunk to remember it.

FRED: Well, let's hope not. I may need them as witnesses.

JANICE: I don't understand.

EDITH: Tell her, Fred.

JANICE: What?

EDITH: Tell her what you've signed.

Pause.

FRED: I've signed a letter condemning the invasion of Hungary as brutal suppression. Saying that it showed Stalinism was alive and well.

JANICE: Sorry? You've signed?

FRED: Yes. I've signed.

JANICE: But in the meeting you were so …

FRED: Correct? Upstanding? Beyond reproach? It was all an act to try to delay the inevitable.

Pause.

JANICE: And you told her first.

FRED: Yes.

JANICE: And that's why she's here. That's why she's turned up again. Because she's convinced you to betray everything you believe in. Just like she has.

EDITH: Fred. It's the right thing to do.

JANICE: He will be expelled. For factionalism. Which is about as bad as you can get.

FRED: Do you think they'll ask me to be present at any meeting that expels me?

EDITH: You really think they'll expel you?

> FRED *looks at her with fear.*

JANICE: They will demand the keys for the new Party car. They will arrive with an empty suitcase and demand every document. That is how it's been done to others who have signed against Hungary.

EDITH: But you've worked for the Party for what …?

FRED: Thirty-five years.

EDITH: Then you should get in first and resign.

FRED: Resigning one's commission is the equivalent to disobeying an order in some armies.

EDITH: But if they're going to expel you …

FRED: I've never done anything else with my life other than Party business, socialism, from the time I wake in the morning until I'm asleep.

JANICE: Why did you sign?

> *Pause.*

FRED: In Budapest, the students took a manifesto for reform to a radio station and requested it be broadcast. They'd elected a twelve-year-old girl to read out their requests. The secret police arrived and shot her through the head.

JANICE: I can't take any more of this.

> JANICE *moves to the other side of the stage.*

> EDITH *takes* FRED's *hand, caressing it.*

FRED: Edith, I wasn't fighting to change the government. I was fighting to change the world, the system, the nature of things.

EDITH: I know.

FRED: The Central Committee is still Stalinist. Here I am terrified they will expel me. If I was in the Soviet they would shoot me or send me to a work camp.

>*Beat.*

I wish they would shoot me.

EDITH: No.

FRED: I have been lied to by people I trusted in the Party. As a consequence I have lied to other people, who trusted me. A lifetime of being lied to and then of spreading the lies.

EDITH: And now you've chosen to stop lying.

>FRED *looks at her.* EDITH *goes over to where* JANICE *is standing.*

Will you resign, when they expel him?

JANICE: I don't think so.

EDITH: Can a member of the Party remain with an expelled member?

JANICE: I've never seen him crack before. He is no longer a deliberate man. Once they lose that, they lose it for good. And if I'm honest with myself, which everyone seems to be urging so persistently, I do want a man who loves the Revolution more than he loves me.

EDITH: You can't walk out on him now.

JANICE: What makes you think you understand the smallest thing about me?

EDITH: I thought we were friends. Family.

JANICE: Listen to you. We're family now you say so. I should be loyal now you say so.

EDITH: It's not just Fred. Thousands of Party members are leaving. Acting on principle, not pragmatism. Remember that, Janice?

JANICE: Fred shouldn't have been an organiser. I would have done it much better. And I should have been sent to China instead of half the bloody men they sent.

EDITH: Sounds to me like you love the chip on your shoulder more than the Revolution.

JANICE: You probably don't want to know this, but as a Party organiser your brother felt he was owed sexual privileges, as part of the elite. He felt it was part of his pay. And he's not the only one.

EDITH: I don't see that in his nature.

JANICE: No, you wouldn't. But then you're a snob, aren't you, Edith? All that use of French in conversation. It's time you stopped playing Lady Edith. Too late to have prevented you contaminating your brother, though.

EDITH: A snob, is it? I think you meant to say decadent bourgeois liberal.

JANICE: If you like. Decadent bourgeois liberal drunk.

EDITH: Not so drunk that I lose control of my vocabulary.

JANICE: No, just so that it anaesthetises your angst. Speaking of which, say hello to your invert when you write to him in England. I know that you'll tell him about all of this. At least that's the excuse you'll use for writing to him behind your current bourgeois husband's back.

JANICE exits.

SCENE SEVENTEEN: ANOTHER TYPE OF BOMBSHELL

EDITH *recites from 'The Rhyme of Joyous Garde':*

EDITH: But I strove full grimly beneath his weight,
> I clung to his poignard desperate,
>> I baffled the thrust that followed,
> And writhing uppermost rose, to deal,
> With bare three inches of broken steel,
> One stroke—Ha! the headpiece crash'd piecemeal,
>> And the knave in his black blood wallow'd.

On the Parliament House lawns.

AMELIA *enters.*

Amelia.

AMELIA: Edith. I see congratulations are in order.

EDITH: Congratulations for what?

AMELIA: The bulldozers at the riverbed. You got them to reinstate the lake into the plans.

EDITH: Well, it was the Prime Minister who wanted it.

AMELIA: At your urging. Hadn't they dropped it from the budget?

EDITH: Yes.

AMELIA: And?

EDITH: And when Holt came to his office, Menzies goes to the window looks out and says, 'Can you assure me, Harold, that by unanimous consent of the ministers, the item of the million pounds for the lake will be struck back into the Treasury estimates?'

AMELIA: Oh, how marvellous.

EDITH: Not for Holt. Especially when the PM turns to me with a raised eyebrow and says, 'Happy, Berry?'

AMELIA: What a triumph.

EDITH: Yes, and in front of a senior minister who has just been kicked up the proverbial.

AMELIA: What did you do?

EDITH: As soon as I got back to my office I called Overall and told him to get the bulldozers down to the river.

AMELIA: Does he know you're not technically on staff?

EDITH: You saw the bulldozers, didn't you?

AMELIA: Well, I'm really pleased for you. Especially since I have some news that may hurt you, hurt us.

EDITH: Are you having another affair?

AMELIA: No.

EDITH: He was twenty-four years your junior.

AMELIA: Well, passionate love is a splendid thing when it comes along, but a good and happy life is possible without it.

EDITH: One can witness great events and participate in great events.

AMELIA: One can meet and talk with fascinating people who have made history.

EDITH: And one can consummately bungle one's loyalties.

AMELIA: Oh, Edith, don't say that. Not now, not with what I'm about to tell you.

EDITH: I say it to show that there is nothing you can say that can possibly hurt me.

AMELIA: Good. Then you won't mind that I've been offered a position in External Affairs.

      EDITH *palls.*

EDITH: External Affairs? You?

AMELIA: It's just a small job.

EDITH: But how?

AMELIA: It's to teach the young diplomats report writing. It's a temporary position.

      Pause.

EDITH: Well. Of course it is. What makes you think that I would mind?

AMELIA: It's just that it's part of the diplomatic life. In a way.

EDITH: It wasn't even advertised. I didn't see it advertised. So it can't be much.

AMELIA: It really would be beneath you, Edith.

EDITH: Absolutely, I'm too senior, too experienced for that sort of work.

AMELIA: You could never have accepted it.

EDITH: Well, how could you possibly know that, Amelia?

AMELIA: You are upset.

EDITH: I'm not. I'd just rather you didn't presume about what I would or wouldn't do.

AMELIA: Something will be offered. I'll keep my eye out.

EDITH: Why not be the friend you purport to be and help me to face the fact that I've missed the boat? I'm too old to apply for positions. I wouldn't humiliate myself by risking a rejection from External Affairs, so don't bother keeping your eye out.

AMELIA: Oh, Edith.

EDITH: Well done, you.

>EDITH *leans and kisses* AMELIA *on the cheek.*

AMELIA: Thank you, my dear.

>EDITH *looks at her and, unbidden, a sob rises into her throat.*

Oh, dear. I'm so sorry to have to tell you.

EDITH: I'm happy for you.

AMELIA: You're lying.

EDITH: Of course I am. I have so much more experience in foreign affairs after all.

AMELIA: Will you come for drinks?

EDITH: Drinks? I thought it was a temporary position.

AMELIA: Well it is, but Dobson said that it's only the second woman in the Department to be appointed, after her, above the level of clerk. She says that things for women, married or not, are really changing.

EDITH: And isn't that marvellous.

>*Pause.*

AMELIA: Apparently in the early days of the Department, after the war, there was a plan to have a diplomatic uniform.

EDITH: Really?

AMELIA: A dark-green tunic with a high collar, trimmed with oak leaves.

EDITH: How hideous.

AMELIA: There was an argument about whether the oak leaves on the collar should be wattle blossoms. Epaulettes were to be braided with insignia indicating rank. They were to wear narrow trousers with broad satin side stripes and a dress sword.

EDITH: A dress sword for the women as well?

AMELIA *laughs.*

AMELIA: I'm sure you'll get much better gossip about External Affairs in the PM's corridor than we will get, stuck out at Yarralumla.

EDITH: A trivial but curative solace, indeed.

AMELIA *exits.*

EDITH *sits on stage, desolate.*

An ACTOR *enters and begins to sing the anthem of the 1972 Labor election campaign, 'It's Time', very softly.*

ACTOR: [*singing*] It's time for freedom,
    It's time for moving,
    It's time to begin,
    Yes it's time …

During the song other ACTORS *enter, one at a time, joining in the singing, and moving around* EDITH. *Each removes a paper from a desk drawer and sets it alight. This is the burning of files that happened (historically) with the incoming Labor Government.*

The ACTORS *continue to sing the entire song.* EDITH *becomes agitated as she watches. Her following comments are interspersed throughout the singing and burning:*

EDITH: What are you doing?
    But that's history.
    Stop.
    Stop.
    You can't destroy that.
    Stop.
    They belong to history, not the Liberal Party.
    Can you even hear me, stop!

The British atomic tests in Australia need to be on the record.

Well, I won't destroy any files I have.

In fact, I've got files, files of my own.

British memoranda on the tests.

I can and I will enter them into an official file.

What's more I'm going to flag it in a memo to the incoming minister.

A gift for the new government.

You just watch me do that.

Or on second thoughts, don't watch me.

I'll do it without your knowledge.

Official file.

It's just not civil.

SCENE EIGHTEEN: THIS NEW LOT

Gough Whitlam's office in Parliament House.

WHITLAM *and* VICTOR HALL *enter.*

WHITLAM: What's she been doing since Menzies retired?

VICTOR HALL: Not a lot. Little bit of publishing about atomic issues.

WHITLAM: You know half the public servants from that era have said that calling me Prime Minister does not come easily to their lips. Wanted to call me Comrade Gough, I suppose.

VICTOR HALL: Or something even less flattering.

WHITLAM: Mmm. She flagged the British atomic testing dishonesty?

VICTOR HALL: In an official memo to the incoming minister.

WHITLAM: Well. Sam Atyeo commends her.

VICTOR HALL: Yes, I saw that in her file.

WHITLAM: He was Evatt's man at the League.

VICTOR HALL: Will I get her to come in?

WHITLAM: What do you think she can do for us?

VICTOR HALL: Well, you've called uranium the devil's work, Prime Minister, perhaps she can be our devil's advocate.

WHITLAM: Being in government, the devil's work is now our work.

VICTOR HALL: You'll see her?

WHITLAM *nods.* VICTOR HALL *motions* EDITH *to enter.*

She is now dressed in a fabulous business suit.

WHITLAM: *Il nous faut des gens qui parler français ici.* [*To* VICTOR HALL] I've said to Madame Berry that we can do with some fluent French speakers around the place. [*To* EDITH] I may ask you to analyse some French documents. Can you do that for me?

EDITH: *Bien entendu. J'observerai en français et en anglais.* I can. I can be a set of eyes in both French and English.

WHITLAM: When my father was Crown Solicitor he took an interest in the Declaration of Human Rights.

EDITH: I'm aware of your father's work, Prime Minister. I wish I had met him.

WHITLAM: How would you like to be an eminent person?

EDITH: It makes me sound rather old, if not fossilised.

WHITLAM: I should think it also makes you, well, eminent.

EDITH: I shan't quibble.

WHITLAM: Then don't. I need you to go out into the world with Mr Hall and report to me on what is happening at the International Atomic Energy Agency and a number of other places. France. Drop in on Israel and sniff around there. I feel we need to have a fresh but experienced set of eyes. I am sure you also know your way around the traps over there. I want to know whether we can trust the Non-Proliferation Treaty.

EDITH: To practise unremitting suspicion in a diplomatic and urbane way.

WHITLAM: Precisely. Find out what the French think they're doing letting off atomic bombs in our backyard. We're sending a naval ship into the testing area, with the New Zealanders, to Mururoa.

VICTOR HALL: You know we have taken the French to the International Court of Justice about the tests?

> EDITH *nods.*

EDITH: I thought a new government might also have questions about what the last government thought it was doing by allowing the British to let bombs off in Australia's backyard.

WHITLAM: All in good time.

> WHITLAM *looks at* VICTOR HALL *and makes a small gesture of approval. Then he begins to leave.*

EDITH: Thank you, Prime Minister.

WHITLAM: And we won't be discussing proliferation by proxy.

EDITH: No.

WHITLAM *exits.*

One last thing.

VICTOR HALL: Fire away.

EDITH: Will I be travelling on a diplomatic passport?

VICTOR HALL: I should think so. You deserve a red passport and all its privileges. Especially for someone who dressed-down Latham in the Melbourne Club over his High Court vote.

EDITH: How could you possibly know about that?

VICTOR HALL: One of our own must have heard whispers.

EDITH: John was something of a mentor.

VICTOR HALL: We don't choose our mentors in life. And either way, we are the masters now.

VICTOR HALL *shakes her hand and exits.*

SCENE NINETEEN: DOES EROS REMEMBER MY NAME?

EDITH *pulls a red passport out of her suit pocket and strokes it, erotically. She recites from 'The Rhyme of Joyous Garde':*

EDITH: And one trod softly with sandal'd feet—
Ah! why are the stolen waters sweet?—
And one crept stealthily after;
I would I had taken him there and wrung
His knavish neck when the dark door swung,
Or torn by the roots his treacherous tongue,
And stifled his hateful laughter.

Vienna, Austria.

VICTOR HALL *enters and sits at a breakfast table.*

VICTOR HALL: Why is it, Edith, that here in Austria I enjoy the Austrian breakfast, in America I enjoy the American breakfast, in France the French breakfast, yet back home I don't eat breakfast at all? Do you have a theory about that, Edith? About breakfast?

EDITH: No, I have no theory on that. That I recall.

VICTOR HALL: That you recall? [*He laughs.*] I like that.

EDITH: You do not realise, my friend, that in life there is quite a bit of forgetting and relearning. Even the forgetting of what one's opinions were.

VICTOR HALL: Changes of habitat require different diets. Maybe we're symbolically eating the prey of the country we're in.

EDITH: Cheese?

VICTOR HALL: *Touché.*

EDITH: You mentioned a plan for the final session?

VICTOR HALL: It's simple. There are seven reports to be given. I'm in number five position. The Soviet guy—Ulyanov—has got last place, we're going to take it away from him.

EDITH: Are we?

VICTOR HALL: All you have to do is deliver a message to the chair during the fourth report. This message will call me from the dais and, while I'm gone, Ulyanov will be forced to speak in position six. I'll come back and give my report in the last position, which means Australia gets the last word on Inspection and Verification regimes.

EDITH: And we will talk about distrust.

VICTOR HALL: What do you mean?

EDITH: We in the IAEA have to live in a world where all negotiation for nuclear disarmament has to be based on distrust. The IAEA is a body founded on distrust. It validates its existence by developing techniques for verification and inspection and detection by being smarter than any one of its members.

VICTOR HALL: Brilliant.

EDITH: Sooner or later electronics will make it possible to eavesdrop on everything of importance that is happening with uranium and weapon making.

VICTOR HALL: You don't think we'll be called cynical?

EDITH: The old League of Nations dream was for open diplomacy. But there will always be the need for darker arts. The world will always be out of control. And nations cannot be trusted to do the right thing.

VICTOR HALL: I suppose not.

EDITH: No, because the right thing doesn't always coincide with profitability and expansion.

VICTOR HALL: The voice of experience.

EDITH: Who admires experience? Experience and wisdom are just pieces of the past, always in combat with the young and the new. Handsome bodies, animation, clever glamour, smart new ideas, these are the seductive things.

Pause.

VICTOR HALL: So will you do it?

EDITH: I think it is a perfectly appropriate *ruse de guerre*.

VICTOR HALL: A good scam.

EDITH: [*flirtatiously*] I don't know what a scam is.

VICTOR HALL: You can guess what a scam is.

EDITH: I suppose I can.

VICTOR HALL: So why, with me, do you pretend to *naiveté*?

EDITH: No reason. Just checking to see if Eros remembers my name I think.

VICTOR HALL: And does he?

EDITH: I'm not sure.

Pause.

VICTOR HALL: Can we really preach distrust as the saddest of truths?

EDITH: The grandest alliance of my life was based on acceptable distrust. An etiquette of distrust, a respectful way of distrusting. It became almost a style of humour within our lives. Distrust can be witty, respectful even. There can be a loving distrust.

VICTOR HALL: The ultimate paradox.

EDITH: Yes, it was. The ultimate, I mean. The most important, most enduring relationship of my life.

VICTOR HALL: This is your husband?

EDITH: Not my current husband. I've decided to leave him while I've been over here. Did I tell you that?

VICTOR HALL: No.

EDITH: No, this was my second husband. He was a British spy. Not that he ever admitted that to me.

Beat.

Our marriage was like a masked ball, but it served a purpose and made good things happen.

VICTOR HALL: Let's do that, then.

EDITH: What?

VICTOR HALL: Make good things happen. For Australia.

EDITH: Say for global nuclear diplomacy and it's a deal.

Pause.

VICTOR HALL: The speakers will come onto the stage.

> *As the lights change, three* SPEAKERS *come onto the stage and sit behind a desk.* VICTOR HALL *joins them.*

The chair is a woman.

> *The* CHAIRWOMAN *joins them. They enact the scene as they describe it.*

When you see number four, Dr Lenrie Peters of Gambia, rise to speak—

EDITH: I shall look cautiously into the conference room.

VICTOR HALL: I'll give you the nod.

EDITH: And I will sidle into the room. Slightly crouched to avoid crossing the line of sight.

VICTOR HALL: You'll pass me without a glance and hand the sealed note addressed to me to the chairwoman.

EDITH: Then I'll turn in a calculated way and, like a fashion model, I'll control my pacing as I cross the dais, glancing only for a moment at the all-male audience as they look at my beautifully tailored clothing.

VICTOR HALL: The chairwoman will read the name on the note and pass it to me. I will frown and put the note in my pocket. Then I will get up, speak to the chairwoman who will look at her watch, nod in an irritated way, and then I will leave the stage.

> *He crosses to where* EDITH *stands.*

EDITH: The chairwoman will indicate to Ulyanov that he is to speak next. He won't be happy. Oh, he'll be so annoyed.

VICTOR HALL: I'll wait a few moments for him to be well into his speech and then I will return to my place on the dais.

CHAIRWOMAN: I call upon Australia to make the final report.

> EDITH *and* VICTOR HALL *make a small gesture of victory.*

SCENE TWENTY: THE REPUBLIC OF THE MIND

There is the sound of an Israeli war jet overhead. EDITH *and* VICTOR HALL *both duck their heads.*

A hotel in Israel.

The ensemble sings the Hebrew hymn 'Ein Keloheinu' ('There Is None Like Our God').

ALL: [*singing*] *Ein kelohenu,*
Ein kadonenu,
Ein kemalkenu,
Ein kemoshi'enu.

Mi chelohenu,
Mi chadonenu,
Mi chemalkenu,
Mi chemoshi'enu.

Node lelohenu,
Node ladonenu,
Node lemalkenu,
Node lemoshi'enu,

Baruch Elohenu,
Baruch Adonenu,
Baruch Malkenu,
Baruch Moshi'enu.

Atah hu Elohenu,
Atah hu Adonenu,
Atah hu Malkenu,
Atah hu Moshi'enu.

EDITH: Have we completely given up on permission to visit the Dimona reactor?

VICTOR HALL: Secrecy about their nuclear weapons is part of the Israeli military and diplomatic strategy.

EDITH: They still haven't even joined the IAEA.

VICTOR HALL: No, but I've arranged to take a trip up to Beirut. Guest of the Israeli Defence Force. They don't rate any diplomat who hasn't been to an actual war zone. Not that I think you need to comply with that sort of imperative.

EDITH: Oh, I'd love to come to see Beirut again. I was there before the war, the Second World War. Back then I spent many nights in the Kit Kat Club.

VICTOR HALL: Sounds exotic.

EDITH: It was the Paris of the East.

VICTOR HALL: It's just that it's a bit rough up there, Edith. There's a civil war and more going on. One of us should stay alive to make the final report.

EDITH: I've been in tough places and done what would be considered dangerous things in my time, VH. In Beirut I carried a revolver and I had to fire shots once.

VICTOR HALL: Slightly different to this.

EDITH: Well, why don't I decide that for myself. I have to have something to tell the Israeli Prime Minister when I'm across the table from him at the next peace talks.

A man, YIZHAR, *enters.*

VICTOR HALL: Here is the colonel who has offered to accompany me. Colonel, Miss Campbell Berry would like to come with us to Beirut.

EDITH: Hello.

She shakes his hand.

I suppose the Club St George and the Colorado are no longer there?

YIZHAR: Those were the glittering days of Beirut.

EDITH: The glittering days of my life as well. It would mean so much to me to be able to see it again.

YIZHAR: All care, no responsibility. This trip is officially invisible.

EDITH: Of course.

YIZHAR: But you should take your hip flask, Miss Berry, the Colorado is, I'm afraid, likely to be closed.

EDITH: Ah, how sad, and me still wanting to play *ma belle vamp Australienne.*

YIZHAR: Excuse me?

EDITH: A moniker from my beloved. Do you have anyone, Colonel, who you discarded, thinking they were only temporary parts of your life, only to find later that they turned out to be the only people who allowed you to really, authentically be you?

YIZHAR: Why would you leave such a person?

EDITH: Because in middle life, desire can bite you like an ant, like a sting. And when its poison courses into your heart, it is such a fresh marvel, such a blistering sensation in the body, that you saturate in it so quickly you realise that you are in the shallow, stagnant water of your illusions, but by then you have junked your past.

YIZHAR: In a war zone, madame, one tries not to live in the past.

EDITH: Yes, only the old do that. And I have fought and will always fight so hard against that happening.

Lights change and EDITH *pulls on sturdy shoes and a scarf. There is the sound of a car engine and all three are in a moving vehicle in Beirut.*

YIZHAR: I have to repeat that this is dangerous country, even though we are in a non-military vehicle.

EDITH: Whatever happens, we will keep driving.

YIZHAR: That's right.

> AMBROSE, JANICE *and* FRED *enter.* AMBROSE *is in his silk dressing-gown,* FRED *and* JANICE *in their communist outfits.*
>
> *A shot is fired.*
>
> EDITH *goes to the three and performs a slow ritualised dance with each.*

EDITH: [*to* FRED] They set up an armoury at the League for the concierges and guards. I kept the pistol there and sometimes did target shooting in the basement.

> *Another shot is fired.* EDITH *transfers to dancing with* JANICE.

[*To* JANICE] I was disloyal and I betrayed the values of open free love. I bungled my inner life, but I know that now.

> *Another shot.* EDITH *transfers to dancing with* AMBROSE.

[*To* AMBROSE] I have witnessed great events and participated in great events. I have met and talked with fascinating people who have made history. But it is only now, here, *now* that I am in it, however briefly, making history, participating in it. One must give everything to participate. To be in it. So many, *so many* will want you to observe, to commentate, to support those who *are* in it. But you must open your palate to the right stuff. You must stare down the world and see it in a clear, cold light. See what you can achieve despite its cruel calculations of worth. It's not what the world hands you, but what you try to wrest from it. That is all that is valuable. To act, to speak, to make. To live, to live, to live it. Your allegiance must be to the republic of the mind, not to any country or state. The republic of the mind is worth …

> *A final shot.*

… everything.

Blood now pours from EDITH*'s mouth. She slumps to the ground. We watch the life fade from her terribly, terribly slowly.*

Blackout.

THE END

~~The Street~~ presents
Cold Light

By <u>Alana Valentine</u> based
on the novel *Cold Light*
by <u>Frank Moorhouse</u>.

World Premiere Season at
The Street Theatre, Canberra
4 – 18 March 2017

Director: Caroline Stacey
Set Designer: Maria T Reginato
Costume Designer: Imogen Keen
Lighting Designer: Linda Buck
Sound Designer: Kimmo Vennonen
Movement Designer: Zsuzsi Soboslay

With Craig Alexander, Nick Byrne, Gerard
Carroll, Tobias Cole, Kiki Skountzos,
and Sonia Todd as Edith

Supported by

ACT Government

St.

<u>Government partner</u>
ACT Government

<u>Street staff</u>

Artistic Director/CEO	Caroline Stacey
Executive Producer	Dean Ellis
Production & Operations Manager	Linda Buck
Communications	Su Hodge
Ticketing & Customer Service	Ketura Budd
Front of House Team	Daniel Berthon
	Anne Murn
	Christiane Nowak
	Dams
Brand and graphic design	Shelly Higgs
Photographers	Lorna Sim

<u>Street board</u>
Colin Neave OAM (Chair), Alisa Taylor (Deputy Chair)
Henry Kazar (Treasurer), Sue Beitz (Secretary)
Beverly Hart, Jamie Hladky

Synopsis

Cold Light is the final novel in Frank Moorhouse's epic trilogy, centred on the flamboyant and ambitious Edith Campbell Berry. Returning from the heady freedoms and liberal tolerance of post-war Europe, Edith and her husband Ambrose Westwood slam into conservative 1950's Canberra with a thud.

With all her experience working at the League of Nations, and with a husband in the diplomatic service, Edith thinks it won't be long until she is snapped up to work as an Australian ambassador or similar prestige public service position. But Edith has a wait on her hands. Her communist brother, Frederick, with whom she is now reacquainted, and his girlfriend Janice, appeal to her to help their cause, which greatly interests the newly formed ASIO. Ambrose, increasingly suffocated by the provincialism of the new Australian capital, longs to put on a frock in public and then does, with disastrous results. Finally, Edith must face the challenge presented to all vivacious, sensuous bohemians living an alternative life in a straight-laced town, the promise of lust and more with a man who may just give her the social acceptance she needs to succeed.

An epic sweep of Australian history, studded with real-life characters, which moves into Edith's reinvention in the Whitlam era, *Cold Light* is both a cautionary tale and a poignant insight into the tension between personal promise and the availability of social opportunity.

The acts

Act One

This Life-Stream Thin
The Outermost Brink
Something Like a Welsh Miner
The Power of Ill-definition
The Costumes Money Wears
Mister Spotless
Some Suggestion of Passion
What Fresh Hell
Protégé No Longer

Act Two

The Radicalism of its Time
Bloomsbury on the Molonglo
Spinning the World On One's Thumb
Declaration of The Free
My Brother's Keeper
Mount Bleakness in the Garden
No longer a Deliberate Man
Another Type of Bombshell
This New Lot
Does Eros Remember My Name?
The Republic of The Mind

This production runs for approximately 140 minutes including an interval.

The scenes

The action of the play takes place over twenty four years from 1950 to 1974 and traverses a series of locations including: The Lodge; a private suite at the Hotel Canberra; town planner Trevor Gibson's offices, Acton; a café in Manuka; the Melbourne Club; Berry Cemetery, NSW; Edith and Ambrose's home on Arthur Circle, Forrest; the Commonwealth Club; Edith's office, Acton; Hotel Canberra's Blue Room; Richard's home; University House, ANU; Parliament House lawns; Whitlam's office, Parliament House; Vienna, Austria; a hotel in Israel; Beirut, Lebanon.

Production

Cast (in order of appearance)

Sonia Todd
Nick Byrne
Tobias Cole
Gerard Carroll
Craig Alexander
Kiki Skountzos

Creative team

Director	Caroline Stacey
Set Designer	Maria T Reginato
Costume Designer	Imogen Keen
Lighting Designer	Linda Buck
Sound Designer	Kimmo Vennonen
Movement Designer	Zsuzsi Soboslay
Voice Coach	Dianna Nixon

Production team

Stage Manager	Angharad Lindley
Sound Operator	Kyle Sheedy
Lighting Operator	Samantha Pickering
Set Construction	Steve Crossley
Publicity	Su Hodge
Graphic Design	Mike Jackson (Dams)
Poster Image	Shelly Higgs

We would like to thank the Nicholls Family. The Set Designs and Artwork created by Maria T Reginato are based on the works created by Walter Burley Griffin and Marion Mahony Griffin held at the National Library of Australia from "*The Papers of Walter Burley Griffin and Marion Mahony Collection MS 9957*" collected by Eric Milton Nicholls.

From the Author

The Edith Trilogy was written over twenty years – in Geneva, in France, in Washington DC, in Cambridge, in Canberra, and in places around Jaspers Brush on the NSW south coast, where Edith began her life. My character Edith, in *Cold Light* begins her life as a young Australian trying to make her way in international diplomacy in the 1920s and 1930s at the League of Nations. She had come through this great disaster in human vision — what some saw as the greatest diplomatic tragedy of the 20th century. In *Cold Light* Edith returns to Australia and to Canberra in some personal and professional disarray. In Canberra, she involves herself in the creation of the world's newest capital city of hope, a visionary and controversial project - a city to be 'like no other'.

But in Canberra, Edith again confronts all the great problems of the human race, and her own personal dilemmas, how we organise the way we live, how do we arrange the way we work, how do we share the nation's riches? She is also an older woman trying to understand her sexuality even if it means crossing the borders or trying to live without borders. She and her diplomat husband, who himself has a secret life, find themselves at the centre of a great and crucial espionage scandal unfolding in Canberra. She is a woman who wrestles for her say in the world, she wrestles with alcohol, she strives for a sexual life which fits her personality, and she searches for peace of mind.

One day in the bus travelling through Canberra in a winter mist I had a dazzling revelation. It was that Canberra may well have evolved into the most aesthetically distinctive and functionally satisfying planned city in the world – that Australia had *pulled it off.* It was then I conceived the novel *Cold Light.* I then had a second realisation. Canberra was now completed in the formal sense, the new parliament house was working and the key cultural institutions were pretty much in place. I even entertained the notion that Canberra might be the most beautiful modern city in the world. It is still a work in progress.

I am honoured that The Street Theatre is premiering the wonderful play and that Alana Valentine agreed to write it so brilliantly.

Frank Moorhouse

From the Playwright

I believe in the enormous capability of human beings. In their inventiveness, their resourcefulness and their creativity. I think that at any time, in any society, there are individuals who can solve the problems that a society has, can guide them toward justice and growth, compassion and success. I do not believe these individuals are always or even often given the power to enact their help or vision. I think too often, far too often, the voices of vision, compassion and justice are shunted to the margins to become voices crying in the wilderness, or in our 21st Century context, drowned out by the glut of competing information, opinion and lies.

Frank Moorhouse has written, in *Cold Light*, a remarkable female role model, a profoundly original emotional and intellectual relationship between Ambrose and Edith, and between Edith and the times in which she lives. What the stage offers the novel is the sacred magic of words made flesh. What the stage offers prose is the vitality and beauty of gesture and voice and intonation and the active silence of the actors. And the invention and imagination and surprise of the director and designers. Live theatre offers all the remarkable unspoken and astonishing things that presence and relationship and subtext and situation give us. It is a liberation of characters from a page into physical reality.

I am grateful to Frank for his generous endorsement of and input into the adaptation, and I thank this astonishing cast and creative team. I hope that Canberra audiences will see that in Caroline Stacey they have a visionary artist and leader who has steered this production to an exceptional outcome.

Alana Valentine

From the Director

Over the last eight years The Street has worked to establish and grow a space for the gathering of theatrical ideas and minds providing fertile ground for Canberra to develop a distinctive and strong voice that is part of our national conversation and cultural narrative.

Producing contemporary Australian theatre in Canberra we pursue intellectually provocative, politically challenging, morally complex, inventive storytelling using all the languages of theatre. The *Cold Light* you experience embodies this ambition for our capital. Theatrical storytelling on a grand scale spanning decades, major historical events, fictional characters and people who actually lived, social mores, sumptuary laws, the personal and political. Reflecting our identity, calling us to action to see what we can achieve in the world now, and entering the communal memory of the capitol.

The support of Robyn Archer and the Centenary of Canberra enabled The Street to option the rights to Frank Moorhouse's magnificent novel and commission playwright Alana Valentine to produce this remarkable adaptation traversing the art of femaleness, people of difference, human rights, the transformation of Australia, vision and ambition, destining a nation, and serving the world.

And then an entire community shared our journey developing the work over the last four years, supporting the audaciously talented actors and creative team to bring Edith and this remarkably rich and resonant Australian play to the stage. Thank you Canberra.

Caroline Stacey

Currency Press

Frank Moorhouse is a full-time writer with a growing international reputation and who has written fiction and non-fiction. He has been awarded major national prizes for the novel, the short story, and the essay. He is now best known for The Edith Trilogy of novels which has as its background the emergence of international diplomacy at the League of Nations. *Grand Days* and *Dark Palace*, and *Cold Light* which has as its background the development of Canberra in the 1950s and the discovery of the dreadful power of uranium and its sinister and peaceful potential. His non-fiction includes the significant chronicle, *Days of Wine and Rage* (Penguin, 1980) which charts the dramatic social changes in Australia during the 1960s and 1970s.

Frank Moorhouse studied undergraduate political science, Australian history, English, and media law, history and practice, at the University of Queensland while working as a cadet newspaper journalist in Sydney and as a journalist in rural areas. After becoming a full-time writer, Moorhouse edited literary magazines, and went on to write fifteen books, to script three feature films and three telemovies, and to involve himself in public life, mainly, around writers' issues. *The Martini Memoir* (2005, Random House) is his most recent book.

Moorhouse was made a Senior Fulbright Fellow, a Woodrow Wilson Scholar at the Woodrow Wilson Center in Washington, and given a one-year residency at King's College, Cambridge to permit him to continue work on his large scale, research-based Edith novels. He has been Colonel Johnson Fellow at the History Department of the University of Sydney.

He has won a number of literary prizes including the Australian Literature Society's Gold Medal for *Forty-Seventeen* (which was also named 'moral winner' of the Booker by the London magazine Glitz). *Grand Days* won the Adelaide Festival National Prize for Fiction. *Dark Palace* won the major Australian literary prize The Miles Franklin award in 2001. He was made a member of the Order of Australia for services to literature. He has been awarded an honorary doctorate from Griffith University and a doctor of letters by the University of Sydney.

His work has been translated into French, German, Chinese, Spanish, Greek, Japanese, Serbian, and Swedish.

Biographies

Cold Light

Currency Press

Alana Valentine
Playwright

Alana Valentine recently wowed Canberra audiences with *Letters to Lindy*, the Merrigong Theatre production which toured to Sydney and Wollongong as well as the Canberra Theatre Centre (CTC) in August 2016. The Street Theatre has presented *Head Full of Love* (the QTC production toured to 23 venues nation-wide and won the APACA Drover Award in 2016) and Alana previously worked with director Caroline Stacey on *MP* in 2011. *Butterfly Dandy* played Street Two in 2005.

Alana is again working with Bangarra Dance Theatre in 2017 as dramaturg on *Bennelong* (CTC August 2017) after working with them on *Patyegarang* (CTC 2014) and *ID* (as part of Belong, 2011). In 2014 Alana won the BBC International Radio Competition and in 2013 she won three AWGIE Awards including the Major Award and the Inaugural David Williamson Award for Excellence in Writing for the Australian Theatre.

Her plays *Parramatta Girls* and *Soft Revolution* are on the NSW Drama syllabus and in 2016 she had her first USA production, *Soft Revolution* at Venus Theatre. In December 2017 *Barbara and the Camp Dogs*, co-written with Ursula Yovich, will be presented at Belvoir.

Alana spent extended time in Canberra at the National Library when she received a Harold White Fellowship in 2013. In September 2017 the NLA will publish *Dear Lindy*, a compilation of letters from the Lindy Chamberlain-Creighton collection. Alana's plays are published by Currency Press. Alana will be part of a forum at the CTC at 12pm on 5th March, a satellite event of the Sydney *All About Women* festival at the SOH.

Caroline Stacey
Direction

Caroline Stacey is the Artistic Director/ CEO of The Street Theatre, Canberra's leading creative producer of contemporary theatre and live performance and the creative hub for professional and independent artists. In 2012 Caroline received the Canberra Artist of the Year Award for her outstanding contribution to theatre and the performing arts. Caroline has been nominated many times for Green Room Awards and is the recipient of International Women's Day, MEAA, Canberra Critics Circle and Victorian Music Theatre Awards. Currently Caroline is on the executive of APACA, the Australian Performing Arts Centre Association.

Caroline has an extensive career as a festival and stage director of theatre and opera working for companies as diverse as West Australian Opera, Adelaide Symphony Orchestra, Melbourne International Arts Festival, Castlemaine State Festival, Melba Festival, Sydney Opera House, Queensland Music Festival, Victorian Opera, Adrian Bohm Presents, Melbourne Theatre Company, Canterbury Opera, Melbourne Opera, Saltpillar Theatre, and Downstage Theatre (NZ). Works directed for The Street include: *The Faithful Servant*, *The Chain Bridge*, *MP*, *To Silence*, *The Give and Take*, *Where I End & You Begin*, *Jacques Brel is Alive and Well and Living in Paris*, *Dido and Aeneas*, *Capital*, *Medea*, *The Jade Harp*, *Albert Herring*, *The Six Memos* and *From A Black Sky*.

Sonia Todd
Actor
Edith Campbell Berry

A graduate of the National Institute of Dramatic Art (NIDA), Sonia has worked extensively in television, theatre, and film. Whilst at NIDA, she was one of the group of students (including Baz Luhrmann) who devised the play *Strictly Ballroom* in which she subsequently starred. Sonia is best known for her appearances in *McLeod's Daughters*, *Police Rescue* for which she won an AFI Award in 1991 for Best Performance by an Actress in a Leading Role, *Rake* (Series 1, 2 & 4) alongside Richard Roxburgh and *The Potato Factory* for which she received an AFI Award Nomination. She most recently appeared in a regular role on the long-running series *Home and Away* for the Seven Network and in the ABC series *Janet King*.

Her other notable television credits include *GP*, *Come In Spinner*, *A Country Practice*, *Mother and Son*, *Over The Hill*, *Heat*, *Water Rats*, *Simone De Beauvoir's Babies*, *Halifax F.P.* and *All Saints*.

Sonia's many stage credits include appearances in *The Winter's Tale*, *Les Liaisons Dangereuses*, *The Golden Age* for the Nimrod Theatre Company and *Harold In Italy* for the Sydney Theatre Company. Her other theatre credits include *Hamlet*, *Much Ado About Nothing* and *Table For One*. In 2014 she completed a successful tour of *A Murder Is Announced* directed by Darren Yap to the Canberra Theatre.

Her film credits include *Shine* opposite Geoffrey Rush and *Rescue – The Movie* directed by Michael Carson.

Nick Byrne
Actor
Robert Menzies PM, Scraper, Gough Whitlam, Waiter, George T. McDowell, Yihzar, Party Goer 2

Best known as one of the most prominent Australian figures in the realm of unscripted theatre, Nick performed, directed, and tutored in Gothenburg, Paris, Vienna, Amsterdam and Liverpool UK in 2016. He is Artistic Director of the international festival of spontaneous theatre, *Improvention* and Impro ACT.

After studying Drama at the University of Newcastle, Nick performed in over thirty musicals and plays through the eighties and nineties, working on diverse productions including: *Gulls, Corpse and Sophisticated Ladies*. He has toured to every state in Australia performing *Theatre In Education* productions in over 1000 schools. In Canberra, Nick has appeared in productions for Jigsaw Theatre Company, Old Parliament House, Shortis and Simpson, numerous Impro ACT seasons, and The Street Theatre's *The Give and Take* and *White Rabbit Red Rabbit*. In 2017, Nick will appear at The Street Theatre in William Zappa's adaptation of Homer's *The Iliad*.

©Michele Mossop

Tobias Cole
Actor
Ambrose, ASIO man, Party-goer 3

Green Room Award winner Tobias Cole is one of Australia's most successful countertenors and is driven by a passion for live performance. For over twenty years he has been singing professionally in opera and concerts around Australia, New Zealand, USA and Europe. As artistic director of Handel in the Theatre, Canberra Choral Society and vocal ensemble Clarion, he has programmed well over 50 performances and in recent years has directed a number of music theatre works.

Recent highlights include performing the role of Willy Wonka in a family show he adapted from Roald Dahl's *Charlie and the Chocolate Factory* for the Canberra International Music Festival; with actor William Zappa, performing *The Sonnets Out Loud* at The Street Theatre; and in the Canberra Playhouse directing and performing in *The Vow*, his adaptation of Handel's *Jephtha*.

Gerard Carroll
Actor
Richard, Thomas, John Latham, Victor Hall, Party Goer 1

Gerard is a NIDA graduate and has worked across TV, theatre, music theatre and film over the past 20 years. Gerard most recently appeared as Eamon in the multi-Helpmann Award winning musical *Once* for GFO at the Princess Theatre in Melbourne, directed by Tony Award winner John Tiffany.

TV credits include *The Code 2* (ABC) *Camp* (NBC), *Underbelly: Badness*, *Rake*, *The Kangaroo Gang* (UKTV), *Tough Nuts* (Foxtel), *Home and Away*, *Backberner* and *Australians at War*. On stage, Gerard most recently played the Homeless Man in the acclaimed Hidden Sydney – The Glittering Mile. In addition he created the role of Smokey in the world premiere of *Dead Man Brake* by Alana Valentine at Merrigong Theatre Company. Gerard also created the role of Mr Frog in the musical workshop production of *Do Good and You Will Be Happy* by Hilary Bell and Phillip Johnstone.

He toured Australasia with *Buddy: The Musical* playing Norman Petty as directed by Craig Ilott. Other theatre credits include *Patsy: The Musical,Wind In The Willows, Cymbeline, Anna Karenina* and *Gathering of Vampires.*

Craig Alexander
Actor
Trevor Gibson, Fred Berry, Tock, Eisenhower

Craig Alexander is an actor, writer and producer, known for the emotional depth and humour he brings to his roles. He holds a Bachelor of Arts (Honours) in Acting, and has an extensive history touring throughout regional centres with Riverina based Gearstick Theatre; the company which he co-founded and led as Artistic Director for almost ten years.

His career comprises playing Bernie Litko in David Mamet's *Sexual Perversity in Chicago*, Dracula himself in Kevin Poynter's adaptation of Bram Stoker's Gothic classic and his acclaimed solo performance of *Jacob Marley's Christmas Carol* by Tom Mula.

He's currently developing the multiplatform comedy series *Trainee Bomb Squad* and adapting *Dr Jekyll and Mr Hyde* and *Frankenstein* as solo storytelling performances. Craig's also a father of four, a motorcycle enthusiast, gamer, somewhat-regular meditator, calisthenics practitioner, Wing Chun Kung Fu student, often house-husband and occasionally finds time to sleep...

Kiki Skountzos
Actor
Janice Linnett, Amelia, Woman

Kiki Skountzos is Canberra-born, public-servant-raised, an actor, writer and collaborator. Recent performance highlights include Stevie in *The Goat, Or Who Is Sylvia?* (King Street Theatre), *Something for Cate* (STC Rough Drafts), *Request Programme* (NIDA 2015 Director's Showcase), *Sophocles' Antigone* (PACT Theatre), under the direction of Jordan Best, *Goldilocks and the Three Bears* (Q Performing Arts Centre).

Kiki graduated from the Australian National University in 2005 with a Bachelor of Arts in Anthropology and Art History, securing a graduate position within the public service while moonlighting as an actor. Realising that her penchant for the dramatic was more suited to the stage than an office, she went on to complete an Advanced Diploma of Performing Arts (Acting) at Actors Centre Australia in Sydney. She is a proud member of Equity.

Maria T Reginato
Set Designer

Maria is a designer of sets and costumes, visual artist and educator. She has a Bachelor Visual Arts, University of Newcastle, Diploma Teaching Secondary, WACAE Edith Cowan University. Highlights of her career include working as Education Officer at The Art Gallery of WA, designing for Opera and *The Vagina Monologues*, receiving Victorian Music Theatre Guild Award Costume Design for *Chess*. Her paintings have been exhibited at Bunbury Regional Art Gallery and Newcastle Contemporary Art Gallery.

Her design work includes for Opera: *Lakme* (Canterbury Opera NZ); *Pimpinone* (WA Opera); *Der Kaiser Von Atlantis* and *Albert Herring* (Operalive! VIC); for theatre: *The Good Body* and *The Vagina Monologues* and National Tour (Adrian Bohm Presents); *Mort* (Naked Villainy); *Shifting Heart* and *Jesus of Montreal* (Stark Raven Theatre Co); for musical theatre: *Les Miserables*, (MS Society WA); *Chess* (Ballarat Light Opera Company); *Disney's Alladin* and *Alice the Musical* (Bunbury Young Voices); *Les Miserables*, *Gondoliers*, *Carousel* and *Secret Garden* (South West Opera Company); *Feast of Life* (Bunbury Catholic Diocesan Liturgical Choir).

Imogen Keen
Costume Designer

Imogen has worked in professional theatre production since 1996. From 2009 to 2013 she was resident designer at The Street Theatre completing over twenty productions and design work including: *The Faithful Servant, The Chain Bridge, MP, Where I End & You Begin, The Give & Take, To Silence, Jacques Brel is Alive and Well and Living in Paris, Lawrie and Shirley* and *Dido & Aeneas*.

As a freelance stage designer Imogen has had the opportunity to work on a wide variety of theatre, music and cross-disciplinary productions with many inspiring companies and individuals including: Aspen Island Theatre Company, Coup Canberra, Barking Spider Visual Theatre, Polyglot Theatre, Smallshows, Canberra Youth Theatre, Little Dove Theatre and Urban Theatre Projects. In 2009 and 2011 Imogen received Canberra Critics Circle Awards for Theatre Design and in 2011 received an MEAA Peer Acknowledgement Award. Imogen teaches part time in the Faculty of Arts and Design at Canberra University.

Linda Buck
Lighting Designer

Linda grew up in Canberra. After graduating from Western Australian Academy of Performing Arts (Lighting), Linda worked between Perth and Canberra for companies such as Yirra Yaakin, Black Swan, Canberra Youth Theatre, Jigsaw Theatre Company, The Australian Choreographic Centre, Shortis and Simpson, Women on a Shoestring and the National Folk Festival.

After working at the Brisbane Convention and Exhibition Centre as Head of Lighting and Bunbury Regional Entertainment Centre as Technical Manager, Linda returned to Canberra and the role of Production and Operations Manager at The Street Theatre, first designing lighting for *The Faithful Servant*. Linda has lit performers such as The Waifs, Diesel, Josh Pyke and Bob Evans, The Searchers, Marina Prior, Rhonda Birchmore and Kate Ceberano. Touring shows include Women on a Shoestring's *At the Cross Roads*, Jigsaw Theatre's *Blue Roof* (The Sydney Opera House) and Black Swan Theatre Company and Adelaide Festival Centre's co-production of *Corrugation Road*.

Kimmo Vennonen
Sound Designer

In 2010 Kimmo won the MEAA Green Room Award for creative and innovative sound design. In 1991 his work on Collaborations with Jim Denley won the prestigious Prix Italia for the ABC. He studied immersive sound in a geodesic dome, becoming an ANU Visiting Fellow in the late nineties. He has run Canberra's only music mastering studio at Gorman Arts Centre since 1997.

Designs, for The Street include *The Chain Bridge, Where I End You Begin, Bartleby, All This Living* and *The Faithful Servant*. Other work includes *The Slip Lane* (AITC), *Ghosts in the Scheme* (bigHart), *Verbatim, Antigone* (CYT), *Blue Roof, The Lost Thing*, and *Pearl vs the World* (Jigsaw Theatre). He collaborated with Denise Higgins and Gary Smith on *Vox Nautica* (ANCA), *The Barbed Maze* (CCAS) and on *Anthology* (Morris & Buining) at Westlake.

© Andrew Sikorski

Zsuzsi Soboslay (BodyEcology)
Movement Designer

Zsuzsi Soboslay has been involved in creative collaborations for over 20 years. Her work spans professional and community-based/participatory theatre, dance, music events, scriptwriting, reviewing, and museum curatorial. Throughout 2016, she taught *Master It: Body* classes for actors at the Street Theatre.

Work as an actor includes *The Chain Bridge* (The Street), *Past Present* (SE Arts) and *Under Milk Wood* (Wild Voices). Her solo *L'Optimisme*, on the life of dancer Jane Avril played the NGA and DANscienCE Festivals. She co-directed major concerts with Synergy Percussion at Angel Place (ABC Limelight award) and Carriageworks in Sydney and is a co-creator with the Parramatta Female Factory Precinct Memory Project. Her trilogy *Anthems and Angel,* on the experience of exile, an intercultural collaboration between musicians, actors, visual and sound artists, has been seen in Canberra and nationally with Part III: *The Compassion Plays* premiering at Gorman Arts Centre in 2016.

Dianna Nixon
Voice Coach

Dianna Nixon works as a pianist, singer, actor, director, music director, producer and animateur, and runs a private studio teaching voice and piano. This skill set has seen her complete a huge variety of work around Australia - as artist-in-residence, on major festivals, and with companies large and small - including her long association with *The Street Theatre*. Dianna was awarded a *Churchill Fellowship* in 2012 for her work with *The Developing Voice* and this year adds another role to her diverse workload – that of Artistic Director of the *Canberra Choral Society*.

Angharad Lindley
Stage Manager

Angharad graduated with Distinction from the University of Wollongong in a Bachelor of Creative Arts (Performance).

As Assistant Stage Manager her credits include *The Dapto Chaser* (Merrigong Theatre Company), *Snugglepot & Cuddlepie* (CDP Theatre Producers), *Hamlet* and *Hedda Gabler* (Belvoir). Her Stage Management credits include *Lucy Black*, *The Political Hearts of Children* (subtlenuance), *Opera at the Forum* (Pacific Opera), *Rust and Bone*, *Fireface*, *Music*, *Minus One Sister* (Stories Like These), *Dirty Blonde* (Garnet Productions), *A Butcher of Distinction* (we do not unhappen), *The Lightbox* (Fat Boy Dancing), *Gaybies*, *Deathtrap*, *The Pride* (Darlinghurst Theatre Company), *RENT – The Musical* (Highway Run Productions), *Belleville* (Mad March Hare Theatre Company) and *Resident Alien* (Left Bauer Productions Sydney and Canberra).

She also toured *Songs for The Fallen* (Critical Stages) to the 2015 Brisbane Wonderland Festival and 2016 Sydney Festival as well as *The Dapto Chaser* in its 2016 NSW Regional Tour.

Acknowledgements

The Street would like to thank the Centenary of Canberra, the National Library of Australia, and the following people for their contribution to the development of *Cold Light*: Craig Alexander, Nick Byrne, Peter Cook, Raoul Craemer, Soren Jensen, Belinda McCloy, Caroline O'Brien, David Pearson, Mary Regan, William Zappa, Robyn Archer, Julian Hobba, Sharne McGee, Vicki Gordon, Joshua Bell and Renee Suttleworth (Pictures and Manuscripts Dept, NLA), Shari Blumer, and Chris Freeman for the red passport. We thank the *Cold Light* Ambassadors Circle for their enthusiasm in helping to spread the word and the Museum of Australian Democracy for bringing Frank and Alana together in conversation before the opening.

Street supporters

We thank Street Supporters enabling The Street to continue to create great theatre for audiences and opportunities for artists, including those making a significant contribution to a chosen production of their choice.

Street—Productions
Colin Neave OAM, Michael Sassella

Street—Life ($5,000+)
Michael Adena, Joanne Daly, Econtext

Street—Party ($1,001–$5,000)
Michael Sassella, Tom Davis, Rohan Buettel, Caroline Stacey, Dean Ellis

Street—Works ($501–$1,000)
David and Margaret Williams, Cathy Winters, George Lawrence, John Passioura

Street—Style ($251–$500)
Colin Neave OAM, Andrew Purdam

Street—Wise ($51 to $250)
Angus Algie, Erin Cassie, Amanda Cenin, Benjamin Crowley, Kattarna Davy, Kirsty Douglas, Christine Ellis, Olivia Fyfe, Maria Hawthorne, Mira Hirnerova, Natalie Howson, Peta Ingles, Amy Jenkins, Jack Kershaw, Vicki Lau, Theresa McCormack, Fergus McCowan, Jason Morrissey, Ann-Maree Nygh, Philip Potterton, Elizabeth Swanton, Janet Thompson, Sanie Ymer, Jessica York, Craig Channells, Sophie Clement, William Fleming, Martin Giddings, Helen Musa, Glenda Naughton, Alisa Taylor, Rosamund (Anne) Murn, Maura Pierlot, Cindy Young, Sara Edson, Tony Weir, Nickola Lee, Roland Balodis, Filip Pavlin, Patrick Lockyer, Drew Kruzins, Martin White, Alec Cullen, Ian Rowe, Marina Roseby, Joshua Chevalier-Brine, Peter Humphries, Sam Bryant, Anna Kolber, Mark Bryson, Robert Macklin, Su Hodge, Chris Johnston, Natalie Cooke, Shireen Ahmad

About The Street

The Street is Canberra's leading creative producer dedicated to contemporary performance, and presenting bold work from other places. Inspired by our geography, history and people, we champion creative process alongside finished work; rich dialogue with our community, and in our city of ideas, inquisitive artists who have something to say about the world.

Over 24 years, the company has established itself as an essential part of Canberra's cultural and imaginative life. The Street is committed to supporting Canberra artists through professional development opportunities, artist residencies and masterclasses.

Our home is The Street Theatre in City West, where writers, actors and audiences meet in our three performance spaces and café. The Street is an artsACT's Key Arts Organisation and considered an essential contributor to the well-being of residents in the ACT and artistic vibrancy in the region.

We are dedicated to bringing distinctive and culturally diverse Australian stories to the stage, with many of the finest and much loved creative talent in the region and beyond, including Canberra's diaspora, shining on our stages. Original works have included: *The Faithful Servant*, *The Chain Bridge*, *Pigman's Lament*, *MP*, *Bartleby*, *Where I End & You Begin*, *From a Black Sky*, *Scandalous Boy*, *How to be (or not to be) Lower*, *Johnny Castellano is Mine* (in partnership with Canberra Youth Theatre), *Pea!*, *In Loco Parentis*, and *Very Sad Fish Lady*.

Our 2017 season goes forward staging exciting new works highlighting the art of possibility in live performance.

www.thestreet.org.au

St.

The Street is an ACT arts facility managed by
The Stagemaster Inc, a not for profit community
organisation, supported by the ACT Government.

Poster artwork for the production of *Cold Light*.
The Street Theatre, 2017.